COOK-UP
in a
Trini Kitchen

John Lyons

Scotch Bonnet Peppers

BY THE SAME AUTHOR

Lure of the Cascadura
Behind the Carnival
Voices from a Silk-Cotton Tree
No Apples in Eden: New and selected poems

The Sun Rises in the North (a collection of four poets)

See also www.johnlyons.org

Dancing a Breakaway

COOK-UP
in a
Trini Kitchen

John Lyons

Peepal Tree

501479442

First published in Great Britain in 2009
Peepal Tree Press Ltd
17 King's Avenue
Leeds LS6 1QS
UK

ISBN13: 978 1 84523 082 1

Peepal Tree Press is home of the best in Caribbean and Black British
fiction, poetry, literary criticism, memoirs ans historical studies.

Discover the website at www.peepaltreepress.com

Supported by
ARTS COUNCIL
ENGLAND

CONTENTS

The recipes are interspersed with poems, paintings and anecdotes for you to discover and enjoy.

ACKNOWLEDGEMENTS

I wish to extend my thanks and appreciation to the team at Peepal Tree Press; in particular, Jeremy Poynting for his interest and enthusiasm when I first approached him with the idea for this unconventional book of recipes. His initial response was energising and inspirational. Hannah Bannister's keen interest in the design and general production of *Cook-up in a Trini Kitchen* was a support and encouragement I value highly. A special thanks to Emma Smith for her skilful application to the editing and proofreading of the manuscript.

Heartfelt thanks and appreciation to my dear wife, Jean, for her patient support of my focused single-mindedness, as day after day I was ensconced in my writing shack at the bottom of our garden, scribbling away; my endless chatter about recipes and her clearing up after my enthusiastic bouts of cooking.

My four sons were my first fans. Their sheer enjoyment of my cooking has been inspirational. I thank them for their encouragement and sowing the seeds for the writing of this book. A special thank you is due also to my sister, Marjorie, who is now living in Barbados, and who willingly accepted the role as my consultant for some of the Trinidad traditional recipes.

Last but by no means least, I would like to extend my sincere thanks to all my friends and family who have happily survived my culinary experiments and, I hope, would wish to come back for more. Thank you.

INTRODUCTION

It was my four sons who long ago first sowed the idea of this book. As they became appreciative of the sensual qualities of food I cooked every day for the family, their suggestions that I write a cookery book were often repeated. But in those days of their growing up, I was fully occupied painting, writing and teaching full-time; still, the idea must have lodged itself in the back of my mind.

Years later, as I cooked more often for others, guests at home or members of the Arvon Centre writing courses I was involved in, I began the habit of using a special notebook to plan menus. This was the embryo of this book. In the notebook I recorded the names of guests, the date and composition of dishes in the menu using a format which, for the purposes of *Cook-Up in a Trini Kitchen*, I call JL's Menu Cooking Grid (see Miscellany). This planning added to my sense of enjoyment in making food. I considered texture, colour, the balance of tastes in the sequential order of the courses, and most importantly, designed the menu to the gastronomic preferences of my guests.

The greatest enjoyment always came though with knowing the pleasure that others were having with the meals I cooked. There was a persistent refrain: *John, you should open a restaurant; John, why don't you at least write a cookery book*. I knew that one day I just had to make time to do it. Meanwhile my sons, long flown the nest, began to enjoy cooking for their own families and friends; occasionally I would receive phone calls from them seeking advice on ways to cook certain things which I was enormously happy to give.

The idea for the cookery book finally possessed me with a fervour when I had the idea that it could combine my three passions: painting, writing and cooking. Surfing on this wave of enthusiasm, I proposed the project to Peepal Tree Press and they responded with the same excitement. The real conception took place with that phone conversation, and the creative gestation of *Cook-Up in a Trini Kitchen* began in earnest.

You may ask how I got so passionate about cooking in the first place. Well, after the death of my mother when I was nine, I went to live with my paternal grandmother and my cousin Yvonne in Tobago. My grandmother, Phoebe, was not a well woman. During her bouts of illness, the cooking of meals fell to Yvonne and I. In hindsight, those Tobago years were important in developing what one could grandly call a philosophy of food and cooking techniques. We lived 'green' in those days. We grew everything we needed to eat to remain healthy. It was the only way for poor people to live in the rural abundance of the island of Tobago.

Many years later when I came to England to study art at Goldsmiths College in London, I continued cooking for myself and occasionally sharing my meals with colleagues. As a Trini far away from home, I derived a strange sense of identity and confidence from cooking that drew on memories of childhood and youth. In the creative atmosphere of the college environment (and, oddly enough, being forced into frugality as a result of not having a grant), I began to make connections between food and art and spirituality in very personal ways. Indeed, this was a new dimension of understanding for me. It opened my eyes to the fundamental similarity of all creative art forms and I began to appreciate cooking on an aesthetic level, and revelled in its sensual completeness.

I learned that at the core of the practice of any art, a knowledge of materials and an understanding of what is possible with them is fundamental. The creative use of these materials, on the other hand, is more difficult to define, because it relies on an individual's imagination, intuition, a perception of the sensual qualities of materials/ingredients, plus an aesthetic *je ne sais quoi*. Cooking falls comfortably into this art process. It has also, I am convinced, a spiritual dimension.

To my way of thinking, love is the vital energy which embraces both cook and diner in a pleasurable gastronomic experience: love in the preparation and cooking, love in the eating, love in the serving and sharing. When I lived with my grandmother there was always food to share. I can still hear her saying: *I am a poor woman; if a beggar come to meh door, ah have no money to give im, but ah could always offer im food.* Growing up in an atmosphere like that, it is little wonder that I have such a passion for food and cooking.

This book is idiosyncratic. As I've suggested, it brings together my three passions of art, writing and food. It doesn't pretend to compete with the attractive productions of the professional chef or be a 'complete' compendium of Trinidadian food. As a Trini away from my first home I've continued to borrow and absorb. Perhaps the book should be called *Cook-up in a Trini's Kitchen*, and this itself would be in keeping with our Trini being. We are a multi-ethnic society. Our cooking reflects our past: the Amerindian Caribs who were there before the Spanish arrived, the French who ruled the island until the beginning of the nineteenth century (when the British took over), and the Africans, Indians (Hindus and Muslims), Chinese and Portuguese Madeirans who came, enforced or with varying degrees of choice, to labour on the sugar estates, or the Syrians or Lebanese who came to peddle goods (and later set up some of our biggest stores). From all of these came elements of our cuisine, and no Trini has ever felt shame in borrowing, adapting and calling their own (what we call creolising) whatever may be had in the way of food from their neighbours. That dynamic, rich, cultural intermix is embedded in the very notion of the cook-up. As Trinis we like our picong (piquancy) in both our food and our talk. If there is one thing we are serious about it is our pleasures.

I do hope that *Cook-Up in a Trini Kitchen* is as much a source of culinary inspiration as it is a record of recipes to which great attention to the principles of good cooking has been given. I hope you are encouraged to use the recipes as a starting point for your own creative experimentation. These days all the ingredients in this book may be found in many supermarkets; and in the cities' open markets there are usually stalls selling Caribbean foodstuffs. All that is left for me to say is, enjoy this book for what it is, a book of recipes, poems, anecdotes, drawings and little watercolour paintings. Enjoy!

COOK-UP LIME

THE KITCHEN'S MONOLOGUE

Here comes my life-giver cook
with senses honed for the alchemy
he practises to the clang of saucepans,
the silvery clinking of cutlery
in cluttered cupboard spaces.
He touches my secret places the way
his body moves when he twirls his spoon,
stirs his pots to the rhythm of soca.

He is a gastronome, an expert
in the use of his tongue; he tastes
and meadow buds burst into flower.

I search his face for nuances
of pleasure. He closes his eyes,
licks his lips, and the tremor comes.

SNACKS AND STARTERS

Hey, Why You Slow So?

As a child growing up in Trinidad, saltfish buljol was my favourite breakfast. Mind you, in a poor household, it was a bit of a luxury reserved for the occasional Sunday. Often we ate it with freshly made johnnie bake and a good slice of avocado, known in Trinidad as *zaboca*.

BULJOL FUH BREAKFAST

Buljol fuh breakfast
is ah-hell-of-ah tasty dish;
meh mudder does mek it
wid good saltfish.

How she mek it so tasty,
ah jus dohn know;
it even taste better
wid slice-up tomato
and ah big piece ah *zaboca*.
Ah telling yuh, man,
wen it com to buljol,
meh mudder is a star.

SMOKED HADDOCK BULJOL

This dish is of Portuguese origin, but the name 'buljol' has a French derivation from **brueler** to burn and **gueule**, mouth. **Bruele-gueule**, burnt mouth becomes 'buljol'.

Ingredients

250 g (8 oz) undyed smoked haddock
juice of 1 lemon or lime
½ a medium-sized onion
1 small red chilli pepper, de-seeded and very finely chopped (optional)
2 garlic cloves
2 tbsp freshly squeezed lemon juice
2-3 tbsp cold pressed extra virgin olive oil
freshly ground black pepper (to your taste)
celery salt or sea salt (to your taste)
1 spring onion in snippets
2 free-range hard-boiled eggs

Cooking instructions

1. Put smoked haddock in a shallow saucepan with lid, cover with cold water to which is added the juice of 1 lemon or lime; bring to the boil, turn off heat and leave fish to poach for 7 minutes with lid on.

2. Drain or strain away the poaching liquid. Wash fish in cold water and set aside to cool.

3. Thinly slice the onion. Chop very finely the de-seeded red chilli and 2 garlic cloves. Mix together the onion, chilli and garlic in the dish from which you intend to serve the buljol.

4. Remove the bones, flake the fish and add to the serving dish. Drizzle the freshly squeezed lemon juice and olive oil onto it. Season to your taste with black pepper and celery salt or sea salt. Blend together well.

5. Garnish with snippets of spring onion and slices of hard-boiled egg.

Traditionally, in Trinidad buljol is made with saltfish (dried salted cod). If saltfish is used instead of smoked haddock, much of the salt must be taken away. Soaking the fish overnight in cold water begins this process. Dispose of the overnight salted water. Continue the removal of salt from the fish by poaching it: put the saltfish in cold water, which must be brought to boiling point and turned off immediately, leaving the saltfish in the hot water for two minutes; the hot water is then discarded and the process repeated once more. At this stage enough salt will have been removed. Follow the instructions for stages 3-5 above.

SALTFISH / SMOKED FISH ACCRAS

Accras: a Trini modification of **akara** (Yoruba): a fried African cake made with ground beans.

Eat as a snack or main dish with tomato and green salad accompanied by a glass of chilled dry white wine; or just as an appetizer, or with floats for a delicious breakfast. See floats recipe (p.16).

Ingredients

450 g (1 lb) saltfish (salted dried cod) or undyed smoked haddock
lemon water for washing fish (see Miscellany p.224), plus 4 slices of lemon
½ tsp dried yeast
50 ml (2 fl oz/3 tbsp) lukewarm water
250 g (8 oz) plain white flour
½ tsp bicarbonate of soda
½ tsp ground black pepper
150 ml (5 fl oz / ¼ pt) skimmed or half-fat fresh milk
½ sweet red pepper (capsicum), finely chopped
½ sweet green pepper (capsicum), finely chopped
1 small red chilli, de-seeded and finely chopped
1 medium-sized onion, finely chopped
3 tbsp finely chopped chives
2 tsp fresh thyme
1 free-range egg, beaten
sunflower oil for frying

Cooking instructions

1. Wash saltfish in lemon water. Rinse it twice in cold water. In a saucepan of cold water with 4 slices of lemon, bring the saltfish to the boil, strain and rinse. Repeat this process twice. *(If smoked haddock is used, bring to the boil in cold water with the slices of lemon, turn off the heat and leave to poach for 7 minutes then rinse in cold water.)*

2. When the fish is cold enough, remove skin and bones and flake or chop coarsely.

3. Stir ½ tsp of dried yeast into the lukewarm water. Set aside for 10 minutes, or until yeast froth rises to the surface.

4. While yeast is being activated, sift flour into a mixing bowl, then blend with it ½ tsp bicarbonate of soda and ½ tsp ground black pepper.

5. Make a well in the centre of the flour mixture. Pour in the yeast and milk and beat into a smooth batter. Add the finely chopped sweet peppers, onion, chives, chilli, thyme and beaten egg. To this savoury batter add the flaked or coarsely chopped fish.

6. In hot sunflower oil, fry the mixture in small desired portions until brown, crisp and cooked through. Lay the accras side by side on absorbent kitchen paper for them to remain crisp.

FLOAT

A quick and easy-to-make breakfast; delicious with saltfish accras. See accras recipe (p.15).

Ingredients

7½ g (1½ tsp) dried yeast, or 210 g (7½ oz) fresh yeast
450 ml (15 fl oz / ¾ pt) lukewarm water
1 tsp salt
1 tsp sugar
675 g (1½ lb) plain flour
3 tbsp melted butter
sunflower oil for deep frying

Cooking instructions

1. In 150 ml (5 fl oz / ¼ pt) of lukewarm water sprinkle 1 tsp sugar, stir to dissolve, then sprinkle in the dried yeast or crumble in the fresh yeast. Stir vigorously and set aside until the surface of the mixture is covered with 2 mm of froth.

2. Sift the flour into a bowl and add salt. Stir the yeast mixture again vigorously and pour into the flour along with the remaining 300 ml (10 fl oz) lukewarm water and the melted butter; mix into a soft dough. Knead lightly on a floured surface to a soft, non-sticky texture; adjust with additional flour if needed.

3. Put the dough into a greased bowl. Brush the top with melted butter; cover and set aside in a warm place until it rises to double its size.

4. Shape into small balls and leave to rise again. Roll out into very thin circles and deep fry in hot oil until brown. Its characteristic behaviour in hot oil is to float to the surface as it is being cooked, hence its name.

A GROCER'S JOKE

A chef in a deli sniffed at a labelled jar.
He slowly shook his head;
'there's something fishy
about this caviar,' he said.

'Eggs-actly,' replied the grocer,
a sturgeon expression on his face.

FISH ROE ROLLS
Serves 4

Ingredients

2 packets of puff pastry
3 tins of cod roe
2 tins of herring roe
2 tbsp breadcrumbs
1 garlic clove, finely minced
1 small onion, finely chopped
1 tsp finely minced dill
½ tsp finely minced Scotch bonnet pepper
1 tsp lemon juice
1 tsp sesame oil
58 g (2 oz) butter
1 small free-range egg, beaten
½ tsp black pepper
salt to taste

Cooking instructions

1. Open the tins of roe into a mixing bowl. Add lemon juice, sesame oil, dill, Scotch bonnet pepper, black pepper and salt to taste.

2. Melt the butter in a frying pan on moderate heat. Add garlic and onion; sauté until onion becomes translucent.

3. Add the onion and garlic with the breadcrumbs to the roes. Mix these ingredients well together and put into the refrigerator to firm up.

4. Roll out the pastry on a dry floured surface; cut rectangles 4 inches (10 cm) by 3 inches (7½ cm) from it. Moisten the edges and place 1 tbsp of roe filling in the centre of each rectangle, flatten a little with the spoon, fold over and seal the edges. Brush with the beaten egg. Prick twice with the point of a knife. Bake in a pre-heated oven 205-220°C/400-425°F/gas mark 6-7, turning heat down to 190°C/375°F/gas mark 5 after 12-15 minutes. Bake until golden brown.

RICE CROQUETTES

Only freshly cooked rice, or cooked rice no more than one day old, stored in a sealed container in a refrigerator, is suitable for this recipe.

Ingredients

450 g (16 oz) cooked rice
1 medium-sized onion, finely chopped
1 clove garlic, finely minced
1 celery stick, approx. 7 inches (18 cm) long, chopped
1 small chilli, de-seeded and finely minced (optional)
1 tsp thyme
1 tbsp chopped parsley
1 tsp freshly ground black pepper
2 tsp sea salt
170 g (6 oz) plain flour
1 free-range egg
1 tbsp extra virgin olive oil
150 ml (5 fl oz / ¼ pt) milk
sunflower oil for frying

Cooking instructions

1. Sift flour into a mixing bowl. Make a well and break an egg into it, add milk and olive oil, mix into a batter. Add the onion, garlic, celery, chilli (if being used), thyme, parsley, black pepper and salt; blend well into the batter. Set aside for 10 minutes; after which time, add the cooked rice and mix thoroughly.

2. To make the croquette, heat oil in a frying pan and when hot slip gently into the hot oil tablespoons of the mixture, flattening each one a little with the back of the spoon. When both sides are golden brown, lay each croquette singly on absorbent kitchen paper. Delicious as a snack on its own or with a dipping sauce of your choice.

FRY BAKES AND JOHNNIE BAKES

As children, living with our grandmother in Rockley Vale, a village near Scarborough in picturesque Tobago, fry bakes and johnnie bakes were regularly eaten accompanied by bush tea for breakfast, or as an evening meal with cocoa tea. It was best freshly cooked, sliced open, steaming and smeared with margarine (sometimes with butter as a luxury). We especially enjoyed it with fried jacks or steamed anchovies.

Ingredients

450 g (1 lb) plain flour
2 tsp bicarbonate of soda
1 level tbsp caster sugar
1 tsp fine sea salt
250 ml (8 fl oz / $^1/_3$ pt) coconut milk or water
45 g (1½ oz) butter or margarine
sunflower oil for frying

Cooking instructions

1. Sift the flour into a mixing bowl; add the salt, bicarbonate of soda and sugar. Blend well.
2. Make a well in the flour. Pour in half the coconut milk or water and mix. At this stage, it will form a rough, ragged dough. Continue adding the milk or water a little at a time and mixing until you get a consistency not too wet and sticky, but suitable for kneading.
3. Transfer dough to a floured surface. Pull open the dough and add a small amount of butter, fold over and knead a few times. Repeat this process several times. Dust with flour if necessary during this process. After about 10 minutes the dough should be soft and smooth, leaving your hands clean. Set aside, cover with a damp cloth for a further 10 minutes.
4. Pinch off pieces of dough roughly twice the size of a golf ball. Flatten into circular shapes 2-3 inches (5-7.5 cm) in diameter and fry in hot oil, maintaining a medium heat to ensure they cook through without burning. The aim is to have golden-brown bakes. The bakes do tend to rise to almost double their size as they cook.

For johnnie bakes, follow the above recipe, with one exception: instead of dividing the dough into balls, flatten the entire lump of dough into a flat bread 7-9 inches (18-23 cm) in diameter and bake in a moderate oven, 190°C/375°F/gas mark 5.

BLACK PUDDING BREAKFAST PATTIE

Serves 6-8

A must for black pudding lovers!

Ingredients

225 g (8 oz) black pudding, peeled and coarsely chopped
4 rashers of smoked streaky bacon, coarsely chopped
I medium-sized onion, finely minced
I garlic clove, finely minced
4 large free-range eggs
I tbsp finely chopped chives
I tsp dried thyme
¼ tsp ground nutmeg
I tsp freshly ground black pepper
I tsp finely minced, de-seeded Scotch bonnet pepper
2 tbsp olive oil
I tbsp milk
salt to taste

For pastry

450 g (I lb) plain flour
175 g (6 oz) butter
¼ tsp salt
2 tbsp water
4 tbsp dry sherry
I small free-range egg for glazing

Cooking instructions

1. Make the pastry: Sift the flour into a mixing bowl. Add the salt. Rub the butter and flour together to form a mixture resembling breadcrumbs. Add the sherry a little at a time, then the water; work into a ball. Leave it to rest.

2. Heat the oil in a deep frying pan. When it is hot sauté the onion and garlic. When the onion becomes translucent, add the bacon and the black pudding. Leave to fry gently.

3. Lightly beat the egg with the nutmeg, black pepper, dried thyme, chives, salt and milk. Pour onto the black pudding and bacon, lower the heat and stir once or twice to scramble. Cook for 2 minutes or until it begins to set. Remove from the heat, add 1 tbsp of cold milk to stop the cooking. Taste for seasoning, adjust if needed and set it aside.

4. On a floured surface roll out the pastry and, using a round pastry cutter about 4 inches (10 cm) in diameter, cut circles out of the pastry. At the centre of each circle put about 1½ tbsp of the filling. Moisten the circular edge of the pastry, fold into a half-moon and seal. When all the patties have been made, brush on the beaten egg glaze. Bake in a pre-heated oven at 205°C/400°F/gas mark 6 for 20-25 minutes or until golden brown.

PICONG FRITTERS
(Thin strips of book tripe, marinated, floured, battered and deep fried)
Serves 4-6

Ingredients

225 g (8 oz) book tripe, cut into strips ¾ inch (2 cm) by 3½ inches (9 cm)
4 tbsp flour, seasoned with 1 tsp dried oregano, 1 tsp freshly ground
    black pepper
sunflower oil for deep-frying

For marinade

3 tbsp lime juice
½ Scotch bonnet pepper, de-seeded and finely minced
2 tsp fine sea salt
1 tsp caster sugar
1 tbsp finely chopped fennel herb or 1 tsp ground fennel seed
1 plump garlic clove, finely minced

For batter

115 g (4 oz) plain white flour
1 level tsp baking powder
1 tsp sugar
½ tsp sea salt
1 free-range egg
150 ml (5 fl oz/¼ pt) lager beer
2 tbsp melted butter or olive oil

Cooking instructions

1. Combine the ingredients for the marinade in a mixing bowl. Add the
   strips of book tripe; mix well into the marinade and leave in the refrigerator
   overnight.
2. Thoroughly mix the batter ingredients in another mixing bowl.
3. Remove the strips of tripe from the marinade. Flour a few at a time;
   dip them into the batter and deep fry in hot corn oil or sunflower oil
   until crisp and golden brown. Drain on kitchen paper towels. Serve as
   a side dish or as a starter accompanied by a lettuce and tomato salad
   with a salty-sweet dressing.

ARRAPE

From the Spanish **arepa**, meaning a corn pancake; by origins an Amerindian bread.

Ingredients

For dough

550 g (20 oz / 1 ¼ lb) medium-ground cornmeal
75 g (2½ oz) plain flour
2 tsp salt
3 tsp baking powder
30 g (1 oz / 2 tbsp) butter
30 g (1 oz / 2 tbsp) lard
water for binding

For filling

225 g (8 oz) minced lamb or beef
2 garlic cloves, finely minced
1 medium-sized onion, finely chopped
1 tsp fresh thyme
½ red chilli, de-seeded and minced very fine
1 tbsp chopped chives
½ tsp salt
1 tbsp sugar
2 tsp black peppercorns
3 cloves
2 tsp cumin seeds
300 ml (10 fl oz / ½ pt) water
2 tbsp sunflower oil

Cooking instructions

1. In a frying pan, gently toast the cumin seeds, cloves and black peppercorns. When they begin to release their aroma, transfer to a mortar and pestle, grind to a powder. Add this powder to the minced meat along with the finely minced chilli, chopped chives and salt. Set aside for 20 minutes.

2. In a deep mixing bowl, blend together the flour, cornmeal, baking powder and salt. Add the butter and lard, cut roughly into ½ inch (1 cm) cubes, rubbing them into the flour to resemble breadcrumbs. At this stage add water to bind the mixture into dough. Knead lightly and set aside.

3. In a heavy saucepan or cast iron pot, heat the oil until very hot, stir in the sugar. When it begins to bubble into a reddish brown caramel, stir the seasoned meat in until it is well integrated with the caramel. Add the onion, garlic and thyme; stir for 1 or 2 minutes before adding the water. Cover and simmer over a gentle heat until the meat is tender and the liquid has almost dried up; taste and adjust seasoning if needed. Set aside to cool.

4. Cut from the dough pieces the size of a large egg. Flatten into a circle the thickness of a little under ½ cm (about 4 mm). Put one tablespoon of the meat filling in the centre, moisten the edges and fold over to form a semicircular pie. Press around the edge to seal. Fry in hot oil until golden brown. Set aside to drain on absorbent kitchen paper.

Many years ago as a boy in Port-of-Spain, Trinidad I had my first taste of arrape bought from a pavement vendor. That spicy taste sensation is like an indelible image etched in my memory and as I write this anecdote I can feel my salivary glands begin to flow.

SALT PAIME

From the French **pain de maiz**, but by origins probably Spanish.

Salt paime is a mouth-watering, spicy, Trinidadian delicacy. As a boy I remember being sent to buy paime from a very large woman who was famous in the Laventille neighbourhood for her sweet and salt paime. She belonged to that generation of poor but industrious and enterprising Caribbean women who ran small domestic-based businesses cooking various tasty snacks, and making just about enough money to survive.

Speaking as someone who loves food and cooking, I believe those women with their culinary skills have contributed to the rich cultural tapestry of Trinidad and Tobago. I honour them.

Ingredients

225 g (8 oz) polenta (cornmeal)
115 g (4 oz) grated pumpkin or butternut squash
170 g (6 oz) finely chopped smoked bacon (dry-cured recommended)
1 onion, grated
1 garlic clove, finely chopped
¼ finely chopped Scotch bonnet pepper or a small de-seeded red chilli
1 tbsp finely chopped fresh chives
300 ml (10 fl oz / ½ pt) warm coconut milk
50 ml (2 fl oz / 3 tbsp) melted sunflower margarine
2 tbsp sunflower oil (for brushing onto kitchen parchment)
¼ tsp baking powder
1 tsp caster sugar
1 tsp freshly ground black pepper
salt to taste
kitchen parchment (as a replacement for banana leaves)
kitchen foil

Cooking instructions

1. Put polenta or cornmeal into a deep mixing bowl. Add black pepper, baking powder and sugar. Blend well.
2. Add the grated pumpkin or butternut squash, grated onion, finely chopped garlic, finely chopped chives and Scotch bonnet pepper or red chilli.
3. Make a well in the mixture and pour in the warm coconut milk, melted sunflower margarine, coarsely chopped bacon, and salt to taste; blend well together. The mixture must not be too stiff, or too wet and runny.

Adjust if necessary with coconut milk to obtain the right consistency. Leave it to rest for 30 minutes, until slightly thickened, then stir the mixture well.

4. Place 1 generous tbsp of the mixture in the centre of a rectangular piece of kitchen parchment 18 x 20.5 cm (7 inches x 8 inches) brushed with oil. Flatten to a thickness of 1 cm (a little under ½ an inch) with the back of the tablespoon and fold into a packet. Place the packet, folded side down, onto a piece of foil the same size as the parchment, fold the edges of the foil to seal and completely enclose its contents.

5. Put the packets into a steamer and cook for one hour. Leave to cool while still sealed. Unwrap and serve as a snack.

PASTELLES

From the Spanish **pastel**, a cornmeal crust stuffed with meat; a staple Christmas dish, originally cooked in banana leaves.

Ingredients

For dough

450 g (1 lb) medium cornmeal (polenta)
30g (1 oz) margarine, chopped into pieces
3 tbsp sunflower oil
1 level tbsp fine sea salt
1 level tbsp granulated sugar
500 ml (16 fl oz) boiling water

For filling

900 g (2 lb) minced lamb or beef
2 grated cloves of garlic
3 medium-sized onions, minced
3 tbsp sunflower oil
1 tbsp tomato purée
2 tsp Caribbean Encona pepper sauce
2 tbsp chopped fresh thyme and basil
1 green and 1 red capsicum pepper, finely chopped
2 tsp freshly ground black pepper
2 tbsp chopped raisins
450 ml (15 fl oz / ¾ pt) vegetable stock

Making the dough

Blend in a suitable mixing bowl the cornmeal (polenta), oil, salt, sugar, margarine and 250 ml (8 fl oz) of the boiling water. As the cornmeal absorbs the boiling water, its texture will change. Test between forefinger and thumb for a mixture which is firmly soft, smooth and not sticky. Use the remaining hot water to adjust the texture if necessary.

Cooking the filling

1. Fry minced lamb or beef in 3 tbsp very hot sunflower oil until meat is brown. Add minced onions, finely chopped green and red capsicums, garlic, tomato purée, Encona and sea salt and ground black pepper; stir to blend ingredients and cook for 5 minutes.

2. Add stock, cover with lid, turn heat down and simmer until meat is tender, approximately 45 minutes. Add chopped raisins and chopped fresh thyme and basil. Adjust seasoning. Continue cooking until most of the liquid has evaporated. Set aside.

Putting it together

1. Cut squares of kitchen parchment and kitchen foil 7 inches by 7 inches (18 x 18 cm) amounting to the number of pastelles you intend to make.

2. Brush oil on to the parchment and place a small ball of dough, the size of an egg, in the centre. Pat the dough flat.

3. Spread a damp piece of muslin over the dough. With a rolling pin, continue to spread the dough until thin (½ cm). Do make sure that there is enough parchment around the dough after spreading to make a secure packet.

4. Remove the damp muslin. Put a tablespoon full of the cooked meat in the centre of the flattened dough. Fold the parchment in half, bringing the dough with it.

5. Lift the parchment covering the pastelle and with a slight pressure of your finger seal the edges of the pastelle. Centre the pastelle on the parchment and fold to make a neat, secure packet. Place this packet, folded side down, onto the kitchen foil. Wrap the foil around it and seal tightly. Repeat this process until all the pastelles are made.

6. Put them in boiling water. Cook for half an hour.

7. Drain immediately and place the pastelles singly on a flat surface to cool a little before taking them out of their foil and parchment. Serve or leave to become cold at which point they retain perfectly their shape.

ROTI

A dish that came with the Indian indentured labourers in the nineteenth century, from the Hindi **roti**, bread without yeast; long a staple of all Trinidadians.

Many years ago when I lived in Trinidad I became addicted to roti. In those days, if my memory serves me right, a roti, in the main, was what we call now 'sada roti' or 'simple roti'. They were then the size of a small dinner plate. If you wanted a dhalpurie, the size remained the same and the only difference was the stuffing of spicy coarsely-ground split peas. Decades later when I returned to Trinidad, eager to recapture the pleasurable experience of a Trinidad roti as I knew it, I asked for a roti on the restaurant floor of Long Circular Shopping Mall and was delightfully shocked by the very large size of what was now a dhalpurie; delicious it was too, with my choice of chicken curry which was wrapped in it. How times have changed. The roti I had on that occasion was a sophisticated update of the simple roti I knew as a boy. I would like to think that the simple or sada roti is still being cooked in the home as a nutritious wrap for the varieties of curry for which Trinidad is noted.

SIMPLE ROTI

Ingredients

450 g (1 lb) plain white flour
3 tsp baking powder
½ tsp salt
2 tbsp sunflower oil
400 ml (14 fl oz / ⅔ pt) lukewarm
   water, for mixing the dough
1 tbsp ghee or melted margarine,
   for brushing roti

DHALPURIE

Ingredients

450 g (1 lb) plain white flour
3 tsp baking powder
½ tsp salt
2 tbsp sunflower oil
400 ml (14 fl oz / ⅔ pt) lukewarm
   water, for mixing the dough
3 tbsp butter, for frying the split peas
115 g (4 oz) yellow split peas,
   washed and soaked in water for
   2-3 hours
1 tsp turmeric
1 tbsp ground cumin
2 bruised garlic cloves
58 g (2 oz) butter and ½ tsp ground
   black pepper, for blending with
   fried split peas

Cooking instructions

The dough ingredients for both the simple roti and the dhalpurie are similar and the method of mixing and kneading is the same. The only difference is the ingredients for the dhalpurie split peas stuffing which entails a separate cooking.

1. Sift flour into a mixing bowl. Add baking powder and salt; blend together. Pour in the warm water and oil and mix well. Knead into a smooth, soft, elastic dough (this is achieved after 7-8 minutes' kneading). Rub a little oil over the dough and cover with a damp cloth. Set it aside to relax for half an hour.

2. If you are making **dhalpurie**, while the dough is resting, boil the split peas with the bruised garlic in a saucepan of water until they are just cooked and retaining a little crunch. Fry the split peas in the butter, cumin, turmeric and salt to taste for about 5 minutes. Set aside to cool before blending in a food processor with butter and black pepper. This is the stuffing for the dhalpurie.

3. Knead the relaxed dough for about 1 minute and divide into balls of equal size.

4. For the **simple roti**, gently flatten one of the dough balls into a circle approximately 4 inches (10 cm) in diameter. Spread ghee or melted margarine onto it. Flatten another ball to the same size and place it on the greased side of the first flattened ball. On a floured surface, roll out the twinned dough as one into a thin circular shape ready for cooking on a tawah or shallow heavy-bottomed frying pan.

5. For the **dhalpurie**, roll out the dough on a floured surface until it is 3½ inches (9 cm) in diameter. Put a generous tsp of the blended stuffing in its centre. Pull the edges over, twist gently to seal and to completely enclose the stuffing. With a rolling pin flatten the dough into a thin circular shape 7-8 inches (18-20 cm) in diameter, ready for cooking. (The technique involved in the making of the dhalpurie at this stage is a case where practice makes perfect; I am still working on it.)

6. For the **simple roti**, cook the first side of each roti for up to 1 minute on medium heat on a slightly greased tawah or shallow, heavy-bottomed frying pan. The roti must not burn and must remain flexible as a wrap for the curry. While this first side is being cooked, brush the uncooked side with a little oil ready to be turned over. Turn. In about 1 minute, when the second side is cooked, insert a knife to separate the two layers and gently pull them apart. Pile the rotis one on top of the other wrapped in a clean kitchen towel.

7. Cook each **dhalpurie** in the same way, but without putting two together as is done in the cooking of the simple roti.

Kneading the Roti Dough

DOUBLES

Short for double baras. **Bara** is a Hindi word meaning a small fried cake of ground pulses.

Ingredients

For dough

225 g (8 oz) plain flour
I tsp turmeric powder
½ tsp ground cumin
½ tsp salt
½ tsp dried yeast, or 8 g fresh yeast
½ tsp sugar
75 ml (4 tbsp / 3 fl oz) warm water
sunflower oil for frying
175 ml (6 fl oz) water for binding

For filling

I tin (240 g / 8½ oz) cooked chick peas
I tbsp curry powder
I onion, finely chopped
3 garlic cloves, finely minced
I small red chilli, de-seeded and finely minced
salt to taste
I tsp cumin seeds
250 ml (8 fl oz) boiling water

Cooking instructions

1. Mix together yeast, sugar and warm water; put aside until yeast froth rises to the surface.
2. Blend together in a large mixing bowl the flour, turmeric powder, ground cumin and salt. Add the yeast mixture and water to bind, then knead into a light, soft dough. Cover with a damp cloth and set aside.
3. While dough is rising, fry in hot oil the cumin seeds, onion and garlic until onion becomes transparent; add the curry powder, stir and cook for I minute then add the chick peas, salt and finely minced chilli, stirring to blend ingredients together.
4. Add the boiling water, cover, lower heat and cook gently until almost all the water has evaporated.

5. Deflate the risen dough with a friendly cuff; knead lightly for about 10-15 seconds then leave it to relax for 10 minutes.

6. Using a tablespoon, scoop off a spoonful of dough, shape it into a ball and flatten into a circle about 4 inches (10 cm) in diameter. Fry in hot oil, turning once. Fry another of equal diameter. Sandwich the curried chickpeas between them to make the popular, delicious 'doubles'. Doubles are delicious served with mango chutney, lime pickle or pepper sauce. It is a famous roadside, fast food snack in Trinidad.

SOUSE

Souse in Trinidad is enjoyed as a snack at parties and during carnival celebrations. It has the well-deserved reputation as a restorative for the seasoned rum boozers. I remember my boyhood experience of Christmas Day in Laventille, the noisy revelries with the bottle-and-spoon percussive rhythms which accompanied the rum-soaked voices giving wild, abandoned renditions of a calypso chorus popular at that time:

> Fire one, neighbour fire one;
> neighbour, yuh so damn deceitful,
> fire one, neighbour fire one…

Christmas was a time to get drunk on rum and make merry with calypso and *winin yuh body*. On occasions such as these, souse came into its own. Revellers had great faith in the spicy-hot souse to pull them away from drunken oblivion.

It is true souse is associated with partying, but it was also often enjoyed for its own sake as a gastronomic delicacy. There were many roadside vendors who set up stalls in the busy parts of towns. They sold souse, black pudding, accras and floats, as well as well-seasoned fried shark. I remember a vendor called Rosie who astutely placed her stall under the awning of a 'rumshop'. In that strategic position she was able to satisfy both serious rum drinkers seeking the salutary, remedial effects of her wares and the customers who just wanted to treat themselves to a delicious snack.

You may well ask, *So what is this 'souse', this rum-drinkers' panacea?* Well, as a dish it has an eponymous characteristic. 'To souse' means to soak in or drench with liquid, and in the context of the recipe which follows, it is about the sousing of certain cooked meats. Ironically enough, the expression *soused* jokingly refers to someone who is thoroughly inebriated.

The taste quality of the sousing liquor is of the utmost importance. It has to achieve a harmonious balance of many ingredients; and it is within this concept of balance that the scope for culinary creativity lies. This is subjective; and is predicated on cook's sensitivity to the subtleties of combining flavours in such a way that they complement each other to create the souse's unique taste.

The following ingredients-list with its measured quantities, if stuck to faithfully, will produce a distinctive flavour; but there is still room for adjustments to suit your taste, especially with the strong flavours.

Ingredients for the sousing liquor

juice of 3 limes
300 ml (10 fl oz / ½ pint) cucumber juice *(this involves fine-grating 2 large cucumbers and squeezing the pulp through a piece of muslin)*
850 ml (30 fl oz / 1½ pt) water
2-3 tsp salt
1 tsp finely chopped Scotch bonnet pepper
1 tsp sugar
1 sweet red pepper, sliced *(a capsicum would do)*
1 sweet green pepper, sliced *(a capsicum would do)*
1 cucumber, peeled and thinly sliced
1 large onion, thinly sliced
2 minced garlic cloves
1 peeled slice of fresh lime

Combine all these ingredients in a large bowl. Stir to blend together. The liquor is now ready to receive cooked meats.

To begin with, the neutral and passive element is water, which will change as the active stronger flavours of salt, lime and pepper give themselves to it. Individually, this trio have strong taste characteristics, but they can be made to work harmoniously together by the cook's culinary skill. Sugar, on the other hand, always plays a reconciliatory role and in controlled quantities can, without being obtrusive, work its magic. Then come what I consider to be the enhancers: finely minced garlic, thinly sliced onions, thinly sliced cucumber. They must live in harmony with the other ingredients to create the complexity of flavours which distinguishes the souse as a really special delicacy. This liquor's purpose is to befriend the cooked meats and subtly complement their tastes. In essence it is an aristocratic marinade with an enobling personality.

Meats to be cooked for sousing

2 lb (1 kg approx.) pig trotters
Remove unwanted bristles then scrub and wash the trotters in lime or lemon water (see Miscellany), cut into small pieces and cook in salted water until tender. When cool, add to souse liquor and leave to marinate in refrigerator for 2 to 3 hours.

1 ox tongue
Clean thoroughly in lime or lemon water. Cook in salted water till tender. Cool and skin, cut into small pieces and add to souse liquor to marinate in refrigerator for 2 to 3 hours.

3 conches, removed from shells
Clean and wash them, leave to soak in ½ pint of lemon or lime juice and water for at least 2 hours. Drain away liquid and cook in salted water until tender. When cool cut into small pieces and add to souse liquor. Leave to marinate in refrigerator for 2 to 3 hours.

4 lb (2 kg approx.) mussels
Scrub and remove beards, steam or drop into boiling, lightly salted water until shells are open. *It is important to discard the unopened ones.* When cool, take them out of their shells and add to souse liquor. Leave to marinate in refrigerator for 2 to 3 hours. You may find it necessary to reduce the quantity of souse liquor.

3 dozen oysters
Scrub and steam them for 3 minutes. Remove from their shells when cool and add to souse liquor. Leave to marinate in refrigerator for 2 to 3 hours. Reduce souse liquor as required.

FISH

A Gift from Uncle Cyril

BONITO IN THE NIGHT

His knocking on our front door,
too loud for the night's silence,
scrambled our montage of dreams; woke us.

There he stood, my wayward uncle-fisherman
silhouetted against stars, a bonito
tensing the muscles of his lifting right arm.

He was passing,
on his way to some God-knows-where place
at that jumbie playtime hour.

Give dis to yuh granmudder, he whispered;
the fish-gift his plea for absolution.

MY CHILDHOOD FISH EXPERIENCE

Living in England, from time to time I yearn for freshly caught fried fish. Even as I write these lines, I unashamedly salivate. Fried fish as I knew it in Trinidad and Tobago was one of the gastronomic benefits (although I did not think so at the time) of the Caribbean Sea which readily yielded a generous supply of a variety of fish.

As a child, I was always present when my grandmother was cleaning fish. It was a performance; I would watch her deftly handling the knife, pushing its sharp point into the fish's pale belly and cutting all the way up to its gills. I looked with horrified wonder at how she pulled away the blood-messy innards of that poor fish. The size of the fish was no problem for her; from sardines to bonito, she gave them the same treatment. Then came the scaling and the flying release of fish scales. They flew everywhere, sticking where they landed. I was never fully out of reach.

The fish was washed in lime water and scrubbed with the lime from which the juice was squeezed. It was surprising how the fishy sea-smell was replaced by the scent of something clean and edible – a sushi smell.

My grandmother used a seasoning of thyme, chives, garlic, Scotch bonnet pepper and black pepper, all crushed together and rubbed into the fish along with salt, lime juice and a touch of vinegar. She was a genius in the way she balanced the seasoning ingredients. Once you tasted her fried fish, steamed fish, or whatever mode of cooking she chose, the experience was unforgettable. But fried fish was my favourite.

Usually the fish was left for several hours (and sometimes overnight) to enjoy a quiet intimacy with the seasoning, after which it was floured and fried in hot oil. That took the smell of delicious cooking to ecstatic heights; anything that smelled that good had to taste good.

COCONUT SMOKED FISH WITH CORNMEAL DUMPLINGS
Serves 4-6

When I was a *shut-tail*, frequent run-away-to-the-neighbour-to-play boy, growing up in Tobago under the stern discipline of my grandmother, coconut smoked fish with cornmeal dumplings was one of my favourite comfort foods. We grew most of what we needed for this recipe.

Our kitchen garden extended far beyond the area surrounding the house. Everywhere there were ground provisions growing with such gay abandon that it appeared as though they sprang up of their own accord, like weeds. My grandmother stood over me, almost six feet tall, a formidable overseer in her broad sunshade, straw hat, arms akimbo on broad hips, while I, with hoe and rake, bullied the dry, hard ground into a condition just right for planting. Often, above the thud and scrape of the hoe, I could hear the happy squeals of my friends, the Douglas children, playing hoop or *What's the Time Mr Wolf?*

On our land we had many coconut trees with a plentiful supply of coconuts, dry and green, all year round. We planted and harvested maize every year. For me, the planting was the easy part. My grandmother dried most of the maize for grinding into cornmeal, which was my job. I hated it.

The mill had the appearance of a customised, iron contraption (see page 136). It was no doubt the product of some wildly creative blacksmith, whom my grandmother, driven by economic necessity, cajoled into making it for her. She was like that, my grandmother. Why buy it, if you could make it yourself, or have it made? It was mounted on sturdy well-seasoned timber. It was a constant irritation to me, that even after years of my pushing-and-pulling effort to produce a fine enough meal for cooking, it remained stubbornly firm and perfectly vertical in its position under our house, which was built on stilts and which generously provided the space for my strenuous activity.

The smoked fish which I recommend for this recipe is really a substitute for what was traditionally used in Tobago. We used what my grandmother called *corned fish*. She had that skill to transform a good chunk of freshly caught fish into corned fish.

Occasionally my uncle Cyril came in the dead of night rapping on the door, loud enough to startle everyone from sleep. There he stood, a tall, unkempt figure on the threshold, holding up by the tail a large bonito which he alone, I believed, had the strength to carry with such little effort. The sight of the fish, however, was usually enough to abort my grandmother's indignation and to earn him an absolution.

After a perfunctory greeting, and while we were still rubbing sleep from our eyes, he was gone as suddenly as he came. We were left wrestling with what was, to my child's eyes, a monster fish. It was freshly caught by the fishermen who managed a fishing vessel in which my uncle had half a share; hence the apparent generosity.

The nights on the island of Tobago were cool enough for us to hang the fish by the tail, with some difficulty, from an upper bolt in the back door of the house, with an enamel plate placed under it on the floor to catch the blood which still dripped from its mouth.

Before the sun had fully risen, that fish had to be gutted, filleted, and salted ready to be laid out in the sun for drying. This was my grandmother's corned fish. We usually did, however, season some of the bonito with salt, Scotch bonnet pepper, thyme, garlic and lime juice. It was left overnight to marinate, ready for frying in the morning. Sometimes we also made fish tea, a sort of fish broth which my grandmother always said was good for the brain.

Ingredients

675 g (1½ lb) smoked haddock or smoked cod, skinned and cut into
    servable portions (*My grandmother's corned fish, as described in the
    introduction to this recipe, would do, if you have the very fresh fish, sun
    and time to make it yourself.*)
lime water (see Miscellany)
850 ml (30 fl oz / 1½ pt) coconut milk, made from two coconuts
1 large onion, sliced thinly
2 garlic cloves, finely minced
3 tomatoes, peeled and quartered
1 small red chilli finely chopped (optional)
1 tsp freshly ground black pepper
1 tbsp fresh thyme
1 tbsp chopped chives
1½ tbsp sunflower oil
1 tbsp lemon juice
salt to taste

For cornmeal dumplings

225 g (8 oz) plain white flour
75 g (2½ oz) cornmeal (polenta)
½ tsp baking powder
1 tsp salt
1 tsp sugar
1 tbsp melted butter
150 ml (5 fl oz / ¼ pt) milk

Cooking instructions for dumplings

Put all the dry ingredients in a mixing bowl; add melted butter and milk. Mix together and knead. At this stage add either a little flour or water as needed to make a sensually smooth, non-sticky dough. Pinch off bits of dough, about the size of a golf ball, roll into a ball and flatten into a circular shape about ½ inch (1 cm) thick. Cook in boiling water. Cooked dumplings float to the surface.

Cooking instructions for fish

1. Rinse smoked fish in lime water, pat dry with kitchen paper towel and set aside.
2. In a deep frying pan, sauté onion, garlic and chilli (if being used) in sunflower oil. When onion turns translucent and soft add the coconut milk. Cook rapidly to reduce its volume to about 250 ml (8 fl oz / ⅓ pint).
3. Add tomatoes and continue to reduce for another 5 minutes. Introduce the fish to the now-thickening sauce to which thyme, chives and black pepper are also added. Lower the heat and gently cook for 10-15 minutes. Taste for salt and add the lemon juice. Serve with cornmeal dumplings.

Eat Yuh Food, Den Yuh Can Play

CURRIED CRAB MEAT WITH HERB DUMPLINGS

Serves 4

Ingredients

3 or 4 crab backs (usually bought ready prepared by the fishmonger)
I onion, finely chopped
2 garlic cloves, finely minced
I tsp tomato purée
I tsp finely chopped chilli (optional)
I tsp black pepper
I generous tbsp curry powder
150 ml (5 fl oz / ¼ pt) coconut milk
300 ml (10 fl oz / ½ pt) water
2 tbsp sunflower oil
salt to taste

For dumplings

225 g (8 oz) self-raising flour
1 free-range egg, beaten, with a dusting of grated nutmeg and ½ tsp of
    ground white pepper
50 ml (2 fl oz / 3 tbsp) milk
2 tbsp melted butter
½ tsp white caster sugar
salt to taste
1 tsp finely chopped chives
2 tbsp coarsely chopped coriander

Cooking instructions for dumplings

Combine all the ingredients in a mixing bowl, using a wooden spoon. When the mixture becomes a lump of dough (if necessary, adjust the texture with a little more flour or water, to achieve a dough that is not sticky and ideal for smooth kneading). Knead for 5 minutes. Pinch off small lumps which you then roll into balls. When you make the balls, allow for the fact that the dumplings will increase in size. Cook the dumplings in lots of boiling water for 10-15 minutes. They float up to the surface when cooked; drain and set aside in a bowl. Drizzle with a little oil; we can't have them 'sticking together', can we! Certainly not in your kitchen.

Cooking the curry

1. In a saucepan with a lid, fry onion and garlic in sunflower oil. When the chopped onion is just turning brown, add curry powder, black pepper, finely chopped chilli and tomato purée. Stir well.
2. Add the coconut milk and water. Turn up the heat to reduce the curry sauce a little, then stir in the crab meat, taste for seasoning and adjust if necessary. Add dumplings, reduce heat and simmer for another 10 minutes. Serve immediately.

KING FISH

My life was never an enviable freedom,
but a knowing in my body of how
to be one with muscular currents of oceans.

So before clouds veil my eyes
and while the fragrance of the sea
still lingers about me,
season me with Scotch bonnet pepper,
salt, dill and lime; cook me with love,
savour my flesh,
be my transmutation.

CURRIED FISH IN PUFF PASTRY

Serves 4-6

Ingredients

675 g (1 ½ lb) white fish, filleted and skinned
lime water for washing, plus 1 tbsp lime juice
300 ml (10 fl oz / ½ pt) milk
1 packet of fresh puff pastry (approx. 500 g/18 oz)
1 large onion, finely chopped
2 garlic cloves, finely chopped
1 tbsp dill, finely chopped
1 tsp chives, finely chopped
1 tsp chopped capers
1 chilli, green or red, de-seeded and finely chopped (to taste)
2 tbsp curry powder mixed with water into a paste
1 tsp black pepper
85 g (3 oz) plain flour
1 tbsp sunflower oil
58 g (2 oz) butter
salt to taste
beaten egg, to glaze

Cooking instructions

1. Wash fish in lime water made with 2 tbsp lime juice and 575 ml (1 pt) water. Rinse in cold water and set aside.

2. In a deep frying pan, fry the onion, garlic and black pepper in the oil and butter on medium heat. When the chopped onion begins to turn translucent, pour in the milk, lay in the fish, reduce heat and allow the fish to poach for 10 minutes.

3. Remove fish, turn up the heat and stir in the curry paste and chilli. As the curry sauce begins to boil, sift the flour in, a little at a time; stir, sift, stir until all the flour is introduced into the sauce. It will begin to thicken; add the dill and chives; taste and adjust seasoning. Add a little extra oil if it begins to stick.

4. Break up the fish into large flakes and, using a wooden spoon, fold them gently into the mixture with the chopped capers and 1 tbsp of lime juice. Turn the heat right down and leave for 2 minutes, then remove from the heat and set aside.

5. On a floured surface, roll out the pastry into a large enough rectangular shape to comfortably accommodate the curried fish filling, and with room for folding and sealing. With the help of the roller, place the pastry into a shallow, greased baking tin of a convenient size. Spoon out the fish filling down the centre of the pastry. Dampen its edges, fold to enclose the filling, sealing along the top and at both ends. With a sharp knife make small slits 1 inch (2½ cm) in length and 3 inches (7½ cm) apart on the top along both sides of the centre seal of the pastry parcel. This is to allow steam to escape while it is being baked. With a brush dipped into a beaten egg, glaze the top and bake in the oven at 190°C/ 375°F/gas mark 5 until golden brown. After baking, allow to cool a little for easy cutting.

CURRIED MUSSELS
Serves 4

Ingredients

2 kg (4 lb) mussels
1 onion, finely chopped
2 cloves garlic, finely minced
58 g (2 oz) butter
1 tbsp sunflower oil
1 tsp sugar
salt to taste
50 ml (2 fl oz / 3 tbsp) single cream (half fat, if possible)
1 tbsp ground cumin
2 tsp turmeric powder
2 tsp plain white flour
1 tbsp garam masala
1 red chilli, de-seeded and finely minced
juice of 1 lime

For fish stock

2-3 fish heads (cod, sea bass, bream)
225 g (8 oz) mussels
lime or lemon water for washing fish (see Miscellany)
1 small shallot, halved
1 tsp black peppercorns
½ tsp fennel seeds
1 tbsp chopped fennel herb
1 tbsp chopped dill
1 tsp sea salt
850 ml (30 fl oz / 1½ pt) water

Cooking instructions for stock

1. Take gills away from fish heads. Wash them in lime or lemon water and leave for 10 minutes in salted water. Rinse thoroughly and put in a saucepan along with the mussels, scrubbed and in their shells; to this add the rest of the fish stock ingredients.
2. Bring to the boil and simmer for 20 minutes. Pass through a sieve lined with muslin. Stock is ready to be used. This recipe requires 300 ml (10 fl oz / ½ pt) of the stock; freeze the rest for future use.

Preparing mussels

1. Scrub the mussels thoroughly, taking their beards away. Discard the ones with broken shells. Cook for two minutes in boiling water with the juice of a lime and 1 tsp salt.

2. Strain when cooked. They should have happily opened up themselves to you. Put aside the ones which have not. When cool, relieve the mussels of their shells. Leave them naked ready to be introduced to the curry sauce.

For curry sauce

1. In a deep frying pan with a lid, first heat the sunflower oil over a medium heat, then melt the butter in the heated sunflower oil and fry, while stirring continuously, 1 tbsp plain flour until golden yellow. Stir in the chopped onion and garlic, cook until soft. Add cumin, turmeric, masala and finely chopped chilli. Stir and cook for 1 minute.

2. First add a little of the fish stock while stirring to make a thick paste; sprinkle in the sugar and add the rest of the stock. Give it a stir and leave to cook and thicken for 5 minutes. Taste and adjust the seasoning.

3. Add the mussels; stir to integrate them with the sauce, turn the heat down and cover, allowing 2 minutes for the mussels to heat through. Add the cream, stir and serve immediately. Curried mussels go well with plain boiled rice or a freshly baked French baguette.

FISH BACCHANAL
Serves 6-8

Ingredients

225 g (8 oz) freshly washed and de-veined prawns
450 g (1 lb) mussels
450 g (1 lb) monk fish, diced into 1½ inch (4 cm) cubes
85 g (3 oz) chorizo sausage, sliced
225 g (8 oz) white crab meat
225 g (8 oz) bulb fennel, quartered
2 garlic cloves, coarsely chopped
1 large onion, chopped
½ small red chilli, de-seeded and finely chopped
2 red capsicum peppers, de-seeded and sliced
150 ml (5 fl oz / ¼ pt) sunflower oil
115 g (4 oz) plain white flour
3 spring onions, chopped
2 tbsp chopped flat leaf parsley (retain the stalks)
150 ml (5 fl oz / ¼ pt) white rum
2 dashes of Angostura bitters
1.1 litre (40 fl oz / 2 pt) light chicken stock
salt to taste

Cooking instructions

1. Examine mussels carefully and discard any with a broken shell. Wash the mussels thoroughly in several changes of water, scrubbing and pulling away their beards.

2. Boil rapidly 300 ml (10 fl oz/½ pt) water in a saucepan with a close fitting lid. Add the mussels to the rapidly boiling water; cover and cook for 2-3 minutes, shaking the saucepan frequently.

3. Tip the mussels into a colander placed over a bowl to preserve their liquor to be added later. Throw away any that have remained stubbornly closed. Remove the rest from their shells and set them aside.

4. Pour 300 ml (10 fl oz/½ pt) boiling water onto the washed prawns. Leave them for 1 minute, then strain them through a sieve over the bowl containing the mussel liquor. After removing their heads, put the prawns with the mussels.

5. Add the prawn heads and parsley stalks to the mussel and prawn liquor; simmer gently to be added later to the chicken stock.

6. Wash the monk fish in a strong solution of lime water; rinse thoroughly and set aside with the mussels and prawns.

7. Make a roux by heating the oil and flour together, while stirring constantly, until it is golden brown. Add the chopped onion, quartered fennel bulbs, finely chopped red chilli, the capsicum peppers and garlic. Cook for 2 minutes. Add the sliced chorizo and stir in gradually the chicken stock together with the strained mussel and prawn liquor and the rum. Bring to the boil and simmer for 20 minutes.

8. Add the monk fish and continue to simmer for another 10 minutes; then let the crab meat, mussels and prawns join in the fish bacchanal. Into this fish *fête*, sprinkle chopped parsley and spring onions; add a couple of dashes of Angostura bitters. Taste for salt and pepper and adjust the seasoning if necessary. This dish is good with anything, but especially with lusty, sticky rice.

FISH CURRIED IN COCONUT MILK
Serves 4

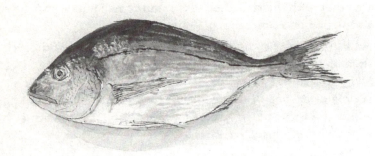

Ingredients

675 g (24 oz / 1 ½ lb) fish: haddock, tilapia, red snapper, or king fish,
    descaled, gilled and rinsed
lime or lemon water for washing fish (see Miscellany)
50 ml (2 fl oz / 3 tbsp) sunflower oil
1 medium-sized onion, chopped
2 garlic cloves, minced
1 tsp finely minced Scotch bonnet pepper (optional)
freshly ground black pepper
2 tsp tomato purée
1 tsp cumin seeds
2 level tbsp ground cumin
1 level tbsp turmeric powder
1 tsp chilli powder
1 tbsp grated coconut cream
1 tin (400 ml / 14 fl oz) coconut milk
1 tbsp lime juice
salt to taste

For marinade

1 tbsp lime juice
2 tsp salt
1 tbsp finely chopped dill
1 tsp finely minced Scotch bonnet pepper
1 tsp freshly ground black pepper
1 tbsp sunflower oil

Cooking instructions

1. Wash fish in lime or lemon water, rinse and pat dry. Cut into good servable portions.

2. Combine the ingredients for the marinade, and marinate the fish portions for at least 15-20 minutes, or preferably overnight.

3. Mix together the ground cumin, turmeric powder and chilli powder to make a basic curry powder.

4. Using a deep frying pan with lid, fry the onions, garlic and cumin seeds in sunflower oil until the onion turns to a light translucent brown. Add 1 tbsp of the curry powder, stir and cook for 1 minute. Put into the mix the black pepper, tomato purée, grated cream coconut and half the coconut milk. Stir to integrate these ingredients.

5. Reduce the contents to the point when the bottom of the deep frying pan can be seen when stirred. Add the rest of the curry powder, cook it for 2 minutes while stirring; then add the rest of the coconut milk and bring to the boil. Turn the heat down to bring this curry sauce to a simmer. Add fish, covering it with the curried sauce and cook for 10-15 minutes. Just before it is removed from the heat, drizzle with 1 tbsp lime juice; taste for salt and adjust if needed. Serve with plain boiled rice.

FISH ESCOVEITCH
Serves 4-6

Ingredients

4-6 fish slices approx. ¾ inch (2 cm) thick
3 limes (use 2 for lime water)
1 tbsp sea salt
1 tbsp freshly ground black pepper
2 large onions, thinly sliced
½ Scotch bonnet pepper, de-seeded and cut into 5 strips
2 tsp allspice grains
1 tsp black peppercorns
½ tsp dried chilli flakes
500 ml (15 fl oz/¾ pt) white wine vinegar
100 ml (4 fl oz/5 tbsp) sunflower oil for frying

Cooking instructions

1. Wash fish in lime water. Pat dry and coat with salt and freshly ground black pepper. Set aside to recover from its surprise at being peppered and salted.

2. Fry slices in hot oil on both sides until crisp. Place them into a deep dish which accommodates them comfortably.

3. Combine all the other ingredients, except the lime, in a saucepan; bring to the boil, then simmer until onion slices are soft. Finally, add the juice of the remaining lime and pour the contents of the saucepan over the fish; leave it overnight to steep in this liquor. This dish makes a wonderful breakfast, eaten cold with freshly baked bread and butter.

FISH ON THE MENU

Your life is centred
in sharp-eyed hunting.
You make of stalking
an elegant art on spindle legs,
every muscle in your body
wound up for the strike.

I have lost that ancient skill:
standing still, feet immersed,
spear held high at deadly angle.

I stalk bargains now
among marble market stalls.
I find not your sticklebacks
but herrings, sprats and jacks
flat and cold as wetland stones.

CHAR-GRILLED TUNA STEAKS WITH SPICY TOMATO SAUCE
Serves 4-6

Ingredients

For fish

4-6 tuna steaks, 1 inch (2½ cm) thick
lemon water (juice of 1 lemon in 450 ml (15 fl oz/¾ pt) water)
2 tbsp olive oil
2 tbsp freshly ground black pepper

For spicy tomato sauce

2 level tsp plain white flour
2 shallots, finely chopped
2 garlic cloves, finely minced
1 tsp freshly ground black pepper
1 tbsp tomato purée
1 tsp caster sugar
1 tsp freshly squeezed lime juice
1 tin plum tomatoes, coarsely processed
2 tbsp coarsely chopped basil
½ tsp balsamic vinegar
175 ml (6 fl oz) vegetable or chicken stock
100 ml (4 fl oz) virgin olive oil
1 whole and intact Scotch bonnet pepper
salt to taste

Cooking instructions for fish

1. Wash steaks in the lemon water. Pat dry with kitchen paper towel and rub with olive oil.

2. Press freshly ground black pepper on both sides of the steaks. Place on a very hot ribbed griddle. Grill for 2 minutes on each side. If griddle is not large enough to grill all the steaks at once, wrap the grilled ones in kitchen foil and keep in a warm place until the rest of the steaks are grilled.

In this recipe the ribbed griddle must be very, very hot. The tuna steaks are grilled for 2 minutes on each side so that they retain their tenderness and flavour. They should always be a little pink in the middle. Because of the quick grilling of the tuna steaks, accompanying dishes, which take a longer time to cook, must be started and nearing completion before the steaks are grilled.

Cooking instructions for spicy tomato sauce

1. In a saucepan over medium heat, fry the flour in 50 ml (2 fl oz/3 tbsp) of olive oil until it becomes a golden yellow. Stir in the finely chopped shallots and finely minced garlic; add the tomato purée, black pepper and sugar. Slowly pour, while stirring, some of the stock to produce a fairly liquid, thick consistency.
2. Add the coarsely processed plum tomatoes, the rest of the stock and the whole intact Scotch bonnet pepper. Cook for 5 minutes.
3. Pour in the remaining 3 tbsp olive oil and the balsamic vinegar. Add the chopped basil; stir and cook for another 3 minutes; add the lime juice, taste and adjust seasoning if necessary. Serve immediately with the grilled tuna. A very tasty and interesting accompaniment to this dish could be a roasted vegetable couscous.

ONE-POT STEAMED FISH AND RICE

Serves 4-6

Ingredients

1 kg (2¼ lb) any filleted fish cut in servable portions, or a whole fish cut
  into slices, and marinated with the following ingredients:
2 tbsp lime juice
2 tsp sea salt
1 tsp freshly ground black pepper
1 tbsp finely chopped dill
1 tbsp sunflower oil and ½ tsp sesame oil if white fish is being used
¼ Scotch bonnet pepper, finely minced (optional)

For rice

450 g (1 lb) long grain rice, soaked in water for 15-20 mins
1 onion, finely chopped
2 garlic cloves, finely chopped
1 green Scotch bonnet pepper, whole and intact (optional)
1 tsp turmeric powder
1 tsp black pepper
2 tbsp olive oil
850 ml (30 fl oz / 1½ pt) vegetable or chicken stock
1 tbsp coarsely chopped parsley

Cooking instructions

1. Drain rice. In a saucepan with a close-fitting lid, fry the rice in olive oil
   for 2 minutes on medium heat. Add the chopped onions, garlic, turmeric
   and black pepper; stir well to integrate the ingredients.

2. Pour in the stock. Stir once to ensure that the grains of rice do not
   stick to the bottom of the saucepan. Add the intact Scotch bonnet pepper
   (this gives a wonderful flavour without adding too much of its characteristic
   pepper heat).

3. When the liquid is reduced to the level of the rice, sprinkle in the chopped
   parsley, remove the Scotch bonnet pepper and place the slices of fish
   on the rice. Cover tightly.

4. Reduce the heat to its lowest position. Cook for another 5-7 minutes.
   The steam trapped in the pan will continue to cook the rice and the
   fish nicely. Serve immediately.

With the best will in the world, the rice in this dish has a tendency to stick to the bottom of the saucepan. As children we called this part of it 'bun-bun'. We regarded it as a delicious treat and often disputed over it. It was crunchy and had all the flavours of the dish concentrated in it. Bun-bun from a pelau pot was particularly prized.

Real convenience food!

PAN-FRIED MACKEREL FILLETS ON WILTED SPINACH
Serves 4

Ingredients for mackerel

4 quarter fillets of a large mackerel
lemon water (see Miscellany), plus 2 tbsp freshly squeezed lemon juice
I tsp Encona pepper sauce
I tsp finely chopped Scotch bonnet pepper (optional)
I tbsp freshly ground black pepper
2 tsp sea salt
3 tbsp corn oil (for frying mackerel)

Ingredients for spinach

250 g (8½ oz) baby spinach
I medium-sized onion, thinly sliced
4 garlic cloves, thinly sliced
58 g (2 oz) butter
I tsp lime juice

Cooking instructions for mackerel

1. Wash mackerel fillets in lemon water and pat dry with kitchen paper towel. Lay them out in a shallow dish. Rub them with salt, black pepper and I tsp finely chopped Scotch bonnet pepper. Drizzle them with the lemon juice and Encona pepper sauce. Set aside for at least 30 minutes.

2. Heat the corn oil in a heavy frying pan until very hot. Lift a fillet out of its marinade, shake off excess liquid and lay it gently on its skin side in the hot oil, with a movement away from you. Fry 2 at a time for 2-3 minutes; the skin should be crisp and golden. Turn and fry the other side of the fillets for another I minute. They are now ready to lie on the spinach bed you have made for them.

Cooking instructions for spinach

1. Put spinach in a large saucepan. Pour about I litre (2 pt) boiling water over the spinach. Leave for approximately 30 seconds, stir, drain through a sieve, pour cold water over it to stop it cooking further. When it is cool squeeze away the residue of water.

2. Gently melt the butter in a heavy-bottomed frying pan. Add the thinly sliced onion and garlic, sauté for I minute. Add spinach, fry for 2 minutes. Drizzle I tsp lime juice, taste for salt, lay the pan-fried mackerel on a bed of the spinach and serve.

SALTFISH WITH OKRA AND TOMATOES
Serves 4-6

Ingredients

450 g (1 lb) saltfish
1 medium-sized onion, coarsely chopped
2 cloves garlic, finely chopped
1 tbsp tomato purée
1 tsp Worcester sauce
1 tsp sugar
1 tbsp plain white flour
4 tomatoes, peeled and quartered
250 g (8 oz) okras, their stem ends trimmed
1 green whole and intact Scotch bonnet pepper
1 tsp freshly ground black pepper
1 tbsp olive oil
25 g (1 oz/2 tbsp) butter
1 tbsp finely chopped fennel herb
300 ml (10 fl oz) water
2 tsp lime juice
salt to taste

Cooking instructions

1. Soak the saltfish overnight. Wash and put in a saucepan with 1 litre (2 pt) cold water. Bring to the boil, simmer for 3 minutes. Drain away water and repeat the process. If saltfish was not soaked overnight, repeat this process twice and rinse with cold water to remove excess salt.

2. Set aside to cool; once cooled, remove bones leaving chunks of fish roughly the size of a tablespoon.

3. Make a roux by frying flour in butter and olive oil in a saucepan over medium heat, while stirring constantly, until golden yellow. Add the coarsely chopped onion and finely chopped garlic; stir to integrate well with the roux. Introduce the tomato purée and sugar to the mix; then, slowly pour in water while stirring. Bring to a gentle boil and add the peeled tomatoes, whole Scotch bonnet pepper and black pepper. Cover and cook to reduce a little.

4. Add the saltfish, the trimmed and washed okras, fennel and Worcester sauce. Simmer for a further 10 minutes; stir in the lime juice and taste for salt, adjust if necessary. Be careful not to damage in any way the now sensitive-to-the-touch Scotch bonnet pepper. Remove with care. Serve this dish immediately with ground provisions (root vegetables, like cassava, sweet potato, eddoes, Tania) or just plain boiled rice.

SULKING MACKEREL

Serves 2-6

Ingredients

2 or 3 mackerel, beheaded, gutted, trimmed and washed in lime or
  lemon water (see Miscellany); then left in salted water for 10 minutes,
  then rinsed thoroughly in cold water
1 onion, thinly sliced
1 tbsp coarsely chopped tarragon
1 tbsp coarsely chopped fennel herb
1 tsp freshly ground black pepper
2 garlic cloves, finely minced
1 tsp freshly grated root ginger
¼ slice Scotch bonnet pepper, finely minced
3 tbsp gin
1 tbsp olive oil
1 tbsp lime juice
1 bay leaf
2 tsp sea salt

Cooking instructions

1. Put all the non-liquid ingredients layered together in an oven-proof casserole
    with a lid. Add the liquid ingredients to the dish.
2. Cook in the oven at a temperature of 190°C/375°F/gas mark 5 for 1
    hour. Serve immediately with boiled potatoes and any green vegetable
    of your liking.

CHICKEN

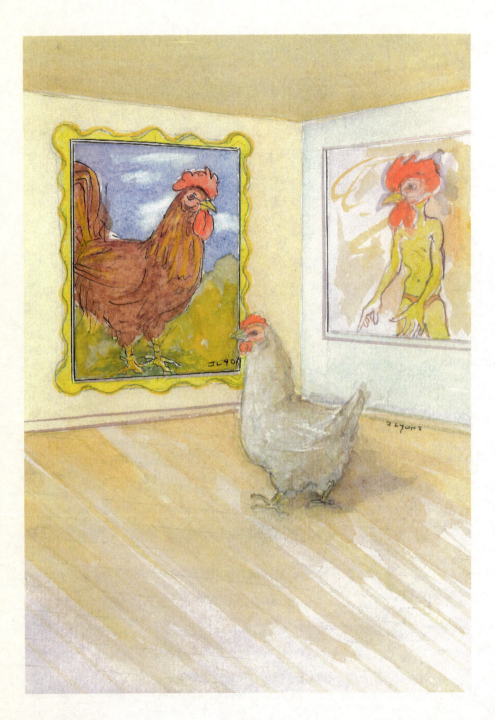

Poulet Morengo

POULET MORENGO

For Toulouse Lautrec

In preparing this dish
what he enjoys most
is making that tame bird
as wild as a coq de bruyère.

He sets it free
from the fowl-run, pursues it
into open country, shoots it
with fine buck shot.

'There must be other ways,
just as quick,
to make a chicken tender,'
his mother often tells him
(and this from an aristocratic
hunting family).

Nevertheless,
she eats heartily his Poulet Morengo,
praises its succulence.

From *Behind the Carnival*, Smith/Doorstop Books

CHICKEN DRUMSTICKS BACCHANAL

Serves at least 1 per person

Ingredients

20 chicken drumsticks
lemon water for washing (see Miscellany)

For marinade

7 cloves
1 tbsp black peppercorns
1 inch (2½ cm) cinnamon stick
1 tbsp coarse salt
½ red chilli, de-seeded and coarsely chopped
3 plump garlic cloves
1 spring onion, coarsely chopped
1 tbsp chives, coarsely chopped
1 tbsp curry powder
2 tbsp water
1 tbsp sunflower or groundnut oil
3 tbsp dark rum
½ tsp Angostura bitters (optional)

Cooking instructions

1. Wash drumsticks in lemon water and set aside to drain.
2. In a small frying pan, dry roast on moderate heat the following: clove, black peppercorns, cinnamon stick and coarse salt. When the spices begin to give off their aroma, transfer to a mortar and pestle or spice grinder and transform into a powder.
3. In a small food processor, make into a paste the garlic, spring onion, chilli and chives.
4. In a small bowl mix together the curry powder, water, oil and ground spices; add the paste to this mixture along with the rum and Angostura.
5. Rub this marinade paste into the drumsticks and leave to marinate overnight. Put in a roasting tin, drizzle with oil, and roast in the oven set at 190°C/ 375°F/gas mark 5. Roast for 45-60 minutes, turning them halfway through roasting. Can be served hot or cold.

CURRIED CHICKEN THIGHS
Serves 4

Ingredients

12 chicken thighs
lemon water for washing (see Miscellany)
2 large onions, coarsely chopped
3 garlic cloves, crushed and minced
300 ml (10 fl oz / ½ pt) chicken stock
1 tbsp cumin seeds
1 piece cinnamon stick (approx. 1 inch/2½ cm)
3 slices root ginger
1 tsp freshly ground black pepper
½ red chilli, de-seeded and finely minced
2 tbsp curry powder
2 tbsp white rum
300 ml (10 fl oz / ½ pt) coconut milk (or 1 tin)
salt to taste
sunflower oil

Cooking instructions

1. Wash chicken in lime or lemon water. Rinse thoroughly and pat dry
    with kitchen towel. Season with salt, black pepper, 1 tbsp curry powder
    and rum. Set aside for at least 30 minutes.

2. In a deep saucepan with a lid, fry coarsely chopped onion in hot oil,
    until translucent and going brown. Add cumin seeds and the other 2
    tbsp curry powder and fry for 3 to 5 seconds while stirring. Add minced
    garlic, ginger, chicken and minced chilli; stir to bring ingredients together.
    Turn the heat down and continue to cook for 10 minutes, stirring from
    time to time. The chicken will begin to spring its own juices; at this
    stage add the stock and coconut milk. Taste for salt and adjust if necessary.

3. Cook at a gentle simmer for 30 minutes with lid on, or until chicken is
    tender. If a thicker sauce is required, cook for another 10-15 minutes
    on a raised heat with saucepan uncovered. Serve with rice, roti or chapati.

PICONG CHICKEN LEGS
Serves 4

Ingredients

4 chicken legs, washed in lime or lemon water (see Miscellany), rinsed
    thoroughly, patted dry
I tbsp Dijon mustard
I tsp caster sugar
½ red chilli, de-seeded and finely minced
2 garlic cloves, finely minced
2 tsp sea salt
freshly ground black pepper
2 tbsp cold-pressed virgin olive oil
I large onion, coarsely chopped
I tsp dried rosemary
I tsp dried thyme
I crushed garlic clove
a sprig of fresh thyme
I whole and intact Scotch bonnet pepper
I tbsp plain flour
450 ml (15 fl oz / ¾ pt) chicken stock
150 ml (5 fl oz / ¼ pt) dry vermouth
30 ml (1 fl oz / 1½ tbsp) single cream (optional)

Cooking instructions

1. In a bowl, mix together as a marinade the Dijon mustard, caster sugar,
    chilli, garlic, salt and black pepper. Rub this marinade into the chicken
    and set aside for at least 1 hour, the longer the better.

2. In a deep saucepan, fry the chicken in olive oil until light brown. Leave
    enough space around the chicken legs to enable them to fry without
    steaming. Remove from saucepan, set aside.

3. Put a little more oil in the same saucepan if needed and fry the coarsely
    chopped onion until soft and slightly brown. Add dried rosemary and
    thyme, crushed garlic, and 1 tbsp plain flour. Stir to integrate well, then
    remove from heat and gradually introduce half of the stock while continuing
    to stir.

4. Add the chicken and vermouth to the saucepan. Pour in the rest of the
    stock, drop in the sprig of thyme and whole Scotch bonnet pepper.
    Taste and adjust seasoning if necessary, cover and simmer until the chicken
    is tender. Remove carefully the Scotch bonnet pepper; put aside for
    intrepid Scotch bonnet pepper lovers. Add single cream if desired. Serve
    with roasted vegetables and herb-butter rice.

SUNDAY CHICKEN STEW
Serves 4-6

Ingredients

1 chicken (1.4-1.8 kg / 3-4 lb)
lime water for washing (see Miscellany)
3 medium-sized potatoes
225 g (8 oz) button mushrooms
1 large onion, chopped
2 garlic cloves, finely minced
1 tbsp finely chopped chives
1 tbsp bruised thyme leaves
2 tsp salt
1 tsp freshly ground black pepper
2 tbsp sunflower or corn oil
1 tbsp brown sugar
575 ml (20 fl oz/1 pt) chicken stock
1 whole and intact green Scotch bonnet pepper
1 bay leaf
bouquet garni of bay leaf, thyme and tarragon (see Miscellany)
2 dashes Angostura bitters (optional)

Cooking instructions

1. Cut chicken into small portions. Wash in lime water. Season with salt, black pepper, bruised thyme leaves, finely chopped chives and half of the minced garlic. Set aside for at least 30 minutes.

2. Peel, wash and cut up the potatoes roughly into 1¼ inch (3 cm) cubes.

3. Heat oil in a large, heavy saucepan or cast iron pot with a lid. When the oil is very hot, add the sugar. As soon as the sugar begins to bubble, put in the chicken and stir vigorously to ensure all the pieces of chicken are well integrated with the caramelised sugar. Reduce the heat a little and cook for 10 minutes with the lid on, stirring from time to time. Add the chopped onion and the rest of the garlic, reduce the heat further and cook for another 5 minutes before adding the mushrooms and potatoes.

4. Add a pint of chicken stock; bring to the boil. Drop in the bouquet garni, whole Scotch bonnet pepper and bay leaf. Stir and reduce the heat; add salt to taste, put the lid on and simmer for 20-30 minutes. When the potatoes are cooked, carefully remove the bouquet garni and Scotch bonnet pepper without rupturing it. Add a dash of Angostura bitters; turn up the heat with the saucepan uncovered to reduce the liquid to a not-too-runny sauce. Taste and adjust seasoning if needed. Remove the bay leaf and serve stew with Trinidad's Sunday rice and peas, boiled plantain and sweet potato.

TRINI COQ AU VIN

Serves 4-6

Ingredients

1 whole chicken (900 g-1.4 kg / 2-3 lb), cut into pieces and washed in
  lemon water (see Miscellany)
85 g (3 oz) smoked bacon (dry-cured, if possible)
½ large onion, coarsely chopped
6 shallots, peeled and left whole
115 g (4 oz) button mushrooms
1 tsp freshly ground black pepper
2 tsp black peppercorns
2 garlic cloves
2 tsp fresh thyme
1 tbsp chopped tarragon
1 tsp balsamic vinegar
2 tbsp olive oil
1 tbsp tomato purée
1 tbsp plain white flour
1 tsp granulated sugar
300 ml (10 fl oz / ½ pt) chicken stock
300 ml (10 fl oz / ½ pt) good, full-bodied, dry red wine
1 tbsp chopped parsley
salt to taste

Cooking instructions

1. With mortar and pestle crush to a pulp the following: 1 tsp coarse sea
   salt, 2 garlic cloves, black peppercorns, thyme and tarragon. Mix in 1
   tsp balsamic vinegar and 1 tbsp olive oil. Rub this seasoning mixture
   well into the chicken pieces and set aside for at least 1 hour.

2. In a deep frying pan, fry in 1 tbsp olive oil the smoked bacon for 2-3
   minutes, then add the chicken and onion. Continue frying until chicken
   begins to turn brown. Add the mushrooms, shallots and freshly ground
   black pepper, stir and cook for another 5-10 minutes, after which, remove
   from heat and transfer into an oven-proof casserole.

3. Put the remaining tablespoon of olive oil into the frying pan in which the
   chicken was fried; add 1 tbsp flour and stir well to form a roux. Put into
   the mix, tomato purée, sugar and a little wine, stirring the while to ensure
   a smooth texture. Add the rest of the wine and chicken stock, cook for
   5 minutes, taste and adjust seasoning, pour over the chicken in the casserole.
   Cover and continue to cook for 45 minutes in the oven heated to 190°C/
   375°F/gas mark 5. Garnish with chopped parsley and serve.

BATTERED CHICKEN
Serves 4-6

Ingredients

6 chicken drumsticks and 6 chicken thighs, washed in lime or lemon
    water (see Miscellany), rinsed thoroughly and patted dry
I bruised clove of garlic
I inch (2½ cm) piece of cinnamon bark
I tsp whole black peppercorns
I sprig of tarragon
50 ml (2 fl oz/3 tbsp) dry sherry
575 ml (20 fl oz/I pt) chicken stock
I free-range egg
225 g (8 oz) plain white flour
I tsp baking powder
I tbsp turmeric powder
I tbsp ground cumin
½ tsp finely minced red hot chilli
175 ml (6 fl oz) lager or soda water
3 tbsp olive oil
groundnut oil or corn oil for deep frying
salt to taste

Cooking instructions

1. In a large saucepan fry the bruised garlic, black peppercorns and cinnamon
    bark in 2 tbsp olive oil. Add the chicken, cook for 2 minutes turning
    the pieces over, with kitchen tongs or a large kitchen spoon, so that
    they come fully into contact with the hot oil. When they begin to turn
    brown, pour into the saucepan the 20 fl oz of stock and the dry sherry.
    Add tarragon and salt to taste. Turn the heat down and simmer for 30
    minutes.

2. Remove the saucepan from the heat. Leave the chicken in the liquor
    to cool and gradually go cold. This process enables the chicken to keep
    moist and retain the enhancing influence of the spices.

3. Beat together in a mixing bowl the egg, flour, baking powder, salt, oil
    and beer or soda water. When the mixture becomes a smooth batter,
    stir in the turmeric, cumin and finely minced chilli; set aside for at
    least 20 minutes to thicken. The batter must not be too runny. It must
    be thick enough to cling to the chicken pieces, covering them fairly
    generously.

4. Remove the pieces of chicken from their liquor and into a sieve or
    colander to drain.

5. Heat in a deep saucepan or wok 2 inches of oil for deep frying. Oil must be moderately hot. In the absence of a thermometer, dropping a cube of bread into the hot oil can indicate the level of temperature: if it browns in 40 seconds, then the oil is at a temperature of about 190°C/375°F/gas mark 5 and just right for this dish.

6. Dip the pieces of chicken into the batter, using tongs, and gently put them into the hot oil. Do not fry too many pieces at once; this lowers the temperature and prevents the batter from becoming crisp. When the pieces are golden brown, remove with a slotted spoon and lay them on kitchen paper in a way that allows air to circulate around them. Laying the pieces one on top of another, or grouped together, creates steam and causes the batter to go soft and soggy. Leave to cool a little before serving.

FREE-RANGE CHICKEN

Yellow fine-feathered balls on matchstick legs,
they lived processing chicken mash
to grow up into pullets with scruffy feathers,
until the open-wire coop and freedom.

As grownup hens they were feisty and wise
always free-range wild with their loving.
Triumphantly they cackled, laid eggs in hides
constructed to their own designs.

Roosters with cockscomb pride stretched necks
for their high-octave coloratura,
flapped their wings and with cockish arrogance

fought off rivals with lethal spurs.
Two cocks in a fowl-yard was one too many.
Hurray for our Sunday chicken stew.

BAKED CHICKEN IN YOGHURT AND MUSTARD
Serves 4-6

Ingredients

1 whole chicken, 675-900 g (1½-2 lb), washed in lime or lemon water
 (see Miscellany), rinsed thoroughly and patted dry
2 tbsp Dijon mustard
4 tbsp plain yoghurt
1 tsp freshly squeezed lime juice
2 tsp freshly ground black pepper
½ tsp fine sea salt
½ tsp freshly ground nutmeg
1 tbsp chopped tarragon
1 garlic clove, finely minced
1 large onion, sliced thinly
150 ml (5 fl oz / ¼ pt) fino sherry
3 tbsp virgin olive oil

Cooking instructions

1. Mix together in a bowl all the ingredients with the exception of the
   chicken, fino sherry, olive oil and onion.
2. Joint the chicken and completely smother the pieces in the mixture of
   yoghurt and Dijon mustard.
3. In a baking dish or casserole with a lid, pour in 1 tbsp olive oil. Lay a
   bed of the sliced onion and place the chicken pieces onto it. Drizzle
   the rest of the olive oil onto the chicken, add the fino sherry. Cover
   and put aside for 30 minutes before putting into the oven. In an oven
   pre-heated at a temperature of 250°C/475°F/gas mark 9, bake the
   chicken for 15 minutes. Lower to 205°C/400°F/gas mark 6 and continue
   to bake for another 45 minutes, or until tender.
4. Remove from the oven and uncover. Test to ensure that the chicken
   pieces are cooked through. Serve with new potatoes and a dollop of
   crème fraîche.

BROWN CHICKEN
Serves 4

Ingredients

1 whole chicken 675-900 g (1½-2 lb)
lemon or lime water for washing (see Miscellany)
Baccra Johnnie chicken marinade (see Miscellany)
1 tbsp brown sugar
3 cloves
2 bay leaf
½ inch (1 cm) cinnamon bark
575 ml (20 fl oz / 1 pt) hot water
2 tbsp sunflower oil
2 tsp salt

Cooking instructions

A particularly watchful eye is needed for the cooking of this dish.

1. Wash chicken in lime or lemon water. Rinse thoroughly and pat dry with kitchen paper towel. Joint the chicken and marinate in Baccra Johnnie marinade for at least 1 hour.

2. In a cast iron pot with a lid, or a heavy saucepan with a lid, heat oil until it is very hot. Add the brown sugar. When the brown sugar begins to caramelise, introduce all at once the marinated chicken; stir vigorously to ensure that all the pieces of chicken are covered with the caramelised sugar. Drop in the cloves, cinnamon, bay leaf and add salt. Cover the pot, lower the heat a little.

3. Keep a watchful eye. The chicken must not burn. To prevent this happening add a little hot water from time to time. Test with a knife to see whether the chicken is cooked through. If juices from the tested piece of chicken run clear without a hint of red, then add no more water and allow the liquid in the pot to go almost dry. The chicken at this stage should be a lovely nut-brown colour ready to be eaten immediately or stored for future meals.

Browning the chicken, as my mother called it, was a way of preserving it for a few days, during the course of which pieces of the chicken would be heated through in sauces in the making of other meals.

SUNDAY-BEST CHICKEN PELAU
Serves 4

Ingredients

1 large chicken 1.8 kg (4 lb)
lemon or lime water for washing (see Miscellany)
85 g (3 oz) pigeon peas
225 g (8 oz) long grain rice, washed thoroughly and soaked for 15
    minutes
140 g (5 oz) carrots, chopped
1 large onion, chopped
1 small onion with 7 cloves stuck into it
1 sprig thyme
1 shallot, peeled
1 whole intact Scotch bonnet pepper (optional)
4 garlic cloves
2 tsp black peppercorns
bouquet garni
'M's Chicken marinade (see Miscellany)
3 tbsp sunflower oil
175 ml (6 fl oz) coconut milk
1 tbsp brown sugar
2 tsp sea salt

Cooking instructions

This dish needs to be prepared in stages: the soaking and cooking of the
pigeon peas; the jointing and marinating of the chicken; the making of chicken
stock using parts of the chicken. These three aspects of the dish must be
done in advance of, or even a day before, the actual cooking of the chicken
pelau.

1. Soak the pigeon peas overnight in cold water. Rinse and put into a saucepan
    of cold water with a bruised garlic clove and the peeled shallot. Cook
    over medium heat until soft, drain through a sieve and set aside.
2. Bathe the chicken in lime or lemon water; rinse and pat dry. Joint the
    chicken into the following pieces: drumsticks, thighs, wings, and the
    whole breast cut into two halves and each half cut into three pieces.
    Set aside the rest for the stock-making. Marinate the chicken pieces in
    'M's Chicken marinade for the duration of time it takes to make the
    stock.

3. To make the stock, chop the rest of the chicken into smaller pieces. Put them in a saucepan with 850 ml (30 fl oz / 1½ pt) of cold water, the small onion with the cloves, 1 clove garlic, black peppercorns and 2 tsp sea salt. Bring to the boil. Drop in the bouquet garni, lower the heat and simmer for 1½ hours. Strain the stock through a sieve and set aside to add to the pelau later.

4. In a cast iron pot or heavy saucepan, heat 2 tbsp sunflower oil until very hot. Add 1 tbsp brown sugar. When the sugar just begins to bubble as caramel, put in the chicken all at once and stir vigorously to ensure that all the pieces are covered with the caramelised sugar. Lower the heat to medium, add 150 ml (5 fl oz / ¼ pt) water, cover with the lid and cook for 20 minutes stirring from time to time. When the liquid has almost dried up, remove from heat. Empty the saucepan of chicken into a bowl.

5. Return the saucepan to the heat. Add the remaining 1 tbsp sunflower oil, the chopped onion, 2 remaining cloves of garlic, finely minced, and the carrots. When the onion begins to turn translucent, add the rice, stir to mix thoroughly with the onion, garlic and carrots. Add 450 ml (15 fl oz / ¾ pt) of chicken stock, the coconut milk, Scotch bonnet pepper and sprig of thyme. Lower the heat, cover with the lid and cook until the liquid is at the same level as the rice. Remove the Scotch bonnet pepper without rupturing it. Stir in the chicken and the drained, cooked pigeon peas, cover, lower the heat even further and cook until liquid is absorbed. Serve immediately.

SCHOOL DINNERS

Ena looks down at her dinner plate:
two scoops of mashed potatoes
looking bored in brown gravy,
a spoonful of green peas
trying to brighten things up.

Ena looks up at the dinner lady:
'Please, please Miss, can I have
chicken pelau or coocoo
and callaloo, tomorrow, please.'

JABMOLASSIE CHICKEN

Named in honour of the Carnival devil character who is covered in pitch oil or molasses (French Creole **jab** = **diable** + **mélasse**). Serves 4.

Ingredients

4 chicken legs (drumsticks and thighs) washed in lime water, rinsed thoroughly and marinated for at least ½ hour in 'M's chicken marinade' (see Miscellany)
1 tbsp molasses
1 large onion, chopped
1 large or 2 small garlic cloves, finely minced
75 ml (3 fl oz / 4 tbsp) dark rum with 50 ml (2 fl oz / 3 tbsp) water
1 tsp finely minced Scotch bonnet pepper
1 whole, intact green Scotch bonnet pepper
1 sprig rosemary
300 ml (10 fl oz / ½ pt) chicken stock
2 tbsp corn oil or sunflower oil
1 tsp paprika
1 tbsp tomato purée
1 tbsp chopped parsley
salt to taste
3 tbsp single cream

Cooking instructions

1. In a heavy saucepan with a lid, or a cast iron pot, fry the chopped onion and finely minced garlic. As the onion becomes translucent, turn the heat right down and add the molasses. Remove the frying pan from heat and stir to integrate the molasses with the onion and garlic.

2. Introduce the chicken legs and the finely minced pepper to the onion and garlic. Turn the chicken pieces to ensure that they are well coated. Return the frying pan or pot to the heat after turning it up. Add tomato purée, paprika and rum with water; stir and continue to cook until the liquid is almost dried up.

3. Add the chicken stock, rosemary and intact Scotch bonnet pepper. Bring to the boil, turn heat right down and simmer for 20-30 minutes. Remove the whole pepper without rupturing it, and the chicken pieces, which must be kept warm.

4. On high heat rapidly reduce the liquor to a thick sauce. Taste and adjust seasoning if needed. Lower heat. Add cream. Return the chicken to the sauce. Stir to coat the pieces of chicken. Serve immediately, garnished with chopped parsley.

DUBROYD CHICKEN SALAD

Named in honour of one of the ships that brought the Chinese to Trinidad as indentured labourers. Serves 4.

Ingredients

225 g (8 oz) very chilled (almost frozen) chicken breasts
1 free-range egg white
1 level tbsp corn flour
1 tbsp light soy sauce
2 tbsp groundnut oil
1 tbsp freshly squeezed lime juice
1 tsp sea salt
½ tsp caster sugar
50 ml (2 fl oz / 3 tbsp) grape seed oil or any light vegetable oil
1 red capsicum, cut in half rings
1 shredded Chinese cabbage
4 free-range hard-boiled eggs, quartered
½ tsp cayenne pepper (optional)

Cooking instructions

1. With a very sharp knife slice the chicken breasts thinly, approximately 3 mm thin. Put into a bowl and sprinkle with light soy sauce. Stir well to ensure that all the chicken pieces enjoy the benefit of the soy sauce. Dust in the corn flour, stirring to cover all the pieces. Stir in the lightly beaten egg white and set aside in the refrigerator for at least 20 minutes.

2. In a wok or large nonstick frying pan, stir fry the chicken pieces, a little at a time, in very hot oil for 2 minutes. Use only 1 tbsp groundnut oil to begin with, add the rest as is necessary during the course of stir-frying. When all the chicken pieces have been stir-fried, set them aside to become cold.

3. In a serving dish, put together the shredded cabbage, red capsicum half-ring slices, hard-boiled eggs.

4. In a small bowl, mix lime juice, sugar, salt and oil. Whisk to an emulsion. Taste for seasoning and adjust to your liking. Add the cold chicken to the serving dish; sprinkle on the lime dressing and cayenne pepper; turn the salad to integrate the ingredients. Serve as a separate dish, or as an accompaniment.

MAH CHICKEN COCOTTE
Serves 4

Ingredients

1 free-range chicken about 1 kg (2¼ lb) jointed into 10 pieces: 2
   drumsticks, 2 thighs, 2 wings, both halves of breast, halved again to
   produce 4 pieces; rinsed in lime or lemon water, patted dry ready for
   seasoning. *The rest of the chicken may be used for stock or chicken soup.*
3 tbsp yoghurt
1 tbsp Dijon mustard
1 tsp freshly ground black pepper
1 tbsp finely minced, de-seeded Scotch bonnet pepper
2 tsp sea salt
1 tsp freshly squeezed lime juice
1 tbsp chives, finely minced
1 sprig of thyme
1 sprig of tarragon
2 cloves garlic, finely minced
1 large onion, finely chopped
3 tbsp extra virgin olive oil
450 ml (15 fl oz / ¾ pt) light chicken stock
salt to taste

Cooking instructions

1. Combine in a mixing bowl the yoghurt, Dijon mustard, ground black
    pepper, Scotch bonnet pepper, sea salt, lime juice and minced chives.
    Rub this mixture into the chicken and set aside to marinate for 1 hour.

2. Heat the olive oil in a large saucepan with a thick base and close-fitting
    lid. When it is quite hot, add the chopped onion, fry until translucent
    and light brown, then add the garlic along with the marinated chicken.
    Cook on high heat for 3-5 minutes, stirring to make sure that all the
    pieces of chicken have come into contact with the oil and that they
    are well integrated with the chopped onion.

3. Add chicken stock, stir and turn the heat up to bring it to the boil.
    Turn the heat right down, cover and simmer for 1 hour.

4. Uncover, taste for seasoning and make adjustments, if needed. Add the
    sprigs of thyme and tarragon. Cook for a further 10-15 minutes to allow
    the herbs to diffuse into sauce. If a thicker sauce is desired, leave the lid
    off, turn the heat up to reduce the sauce. It needs to be closely watched
    at this stage. Serve immediately. It is delicious with sticky herb rice.

CHICKEN WITH TARRAGON AND MUSHROOM SAUCE

Serves 4-6

Ingredients

1 boiler chicken, 800-900 g (1¾-2 lb)
1 medium-sized onion with 3 cloves stuck into it
1 bruised garlic clove
1 intact Scotch bonnet pepper
1 star anise
1 tsp black peppercorns
2 sprigs of fresh and 1 tsp of dried tarragon
1 tsp brown sugar
125 g (4 oz) button mushrooms
2 tbsp plain white flour
½ tsp freshly grated nutmeg
28 g (1 oz) butter
2 tbsp olive oil
250 ml (8 fl oz) dry white wine
salt to taste
water to cover chicken by ½ inch (1 cm)

Cooking instructions

1. Rinse chicken in cold water and place it in a large saucepan with enough water to cover it. Put with the chicken, onion with its cloves, the bruised garlic clove, star anise and black peppercorns. Bring to the boil and simmer for 1 hour.

2. When the chicken is cooked, remove it from the liquor and set it aside to keep warm in a covered dish sat on a saucepan of hot water. Strain the liquid through a sieve, returning it to the saucepan. Add the white wine, button mushrooms, sprigs of tarragon, and Scotch bonnet pepper, whole and intact. Cook until the liquor is reduced to ¾ pt. Remove the sprigs of tarragon and the Scotch bonnet pepper, taking care not to rupture it in any way.

3. In another saucepan heat the olive oil with the butter. Add the flour stirring it into the oil and butter until it becomes a golden brown roux. A little of the reduced liquor can now be added to the roux while continuing to stir. As it thickens, add the rest along with the mushrooms, the freshly grated nutmeg, sugar and dried tarragon.

4. Divide the chicken into servable pieces, adding them to the mushroom and tarragon sauce. Leave to simmer for 10 minutes. Taste and adjust seasoning if needed. Serve immediately with pasta or new potatoes.

MEAT

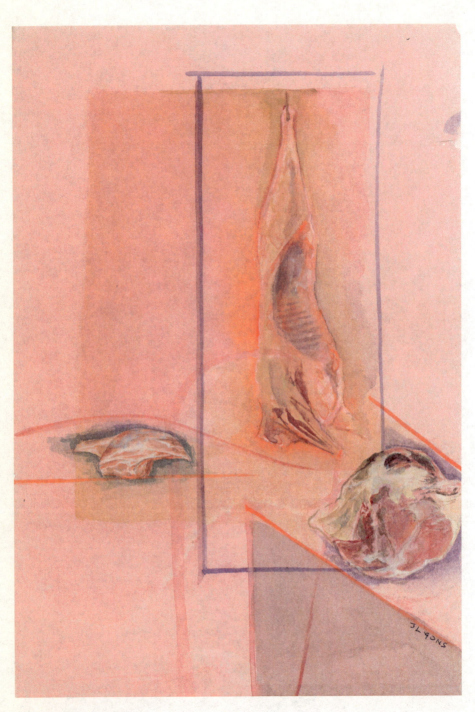

For the Love of Meat

LICK-UP BEEF
Serves 4-6

For this recipe the beef must be marinated beforehand to give it that lick-it-up taste.

To marinate

Mix together in a small bowl 2 finely minced garlic cloves, 2 tbsp grated green paw-paw skin, I tsp finely minced Scotch bonnet pepper, 2 tsp sea salt, I tsp freshly ground black peppercorns, I tbsp sunflower oil and ½ tsp red wine vinegar. Rub this mixture into the beef; marinate for at least 2-3 hours, or preferably overnight.

Ingredients

I kg (2¼ lb) chuck beef
2 sweet red peppers (capsicum), chopped
I large carrot, diced
I tin chopped tomatoes
I tbsp tomato purée
2 tbsp paprika
2 medium-sized red onions, finely chopped
I clove garlic, finely minced
I tbsp plain white flour
I bay leaf
I tsp caster sugar
I inch (2½ cm) cinnamon stick
I sprig thyme
2 tsp freshly ground black peppercorns
50 ml (2 fl oz / 3 tbsp) rum
2 tbsp extra virgin olive oil
58 g (2 oz) butter
300 ml (10 fl oz / ½ pt) vegetable stock
salt to taste

Cooking instructions

1. Cut the marinated beef into 1½ inch (4 cm) cubes.
2. In a heavy-duty saucepan with a lid, or a cast iron pot with a lid, heat the olive oil and butter. When the butter melts, add flour and stir over moderate heat to make a golden brown roux. Put the chopped

onion and minced garlic immediately into the roux and stir to mix thoroughly.

3. Add the beef, stir and cook for 5 minutes; then add the tomato purée, paprika, black pepper, the chopped sweet peppers, carrots, chopped tomato and rum. Stir the mixture well, then add the stock, sprig of thyme, cinnamon and bay leaf; cover the saucepan or pot, lower the heat and simmer for 1½-2 hours, stirring it from time to time. Stir in 1 tsp sugar and salt to taste. Eaten with rice, bread, root vegetables or anything else, I guarantee you will lick it all up.

CREOLE BEEF
Serves 4

Ingredients

450 g (1 lb) chuck beef, briefly rinsed, patted dry and cut into thin slices,
  then strips 1½ cm (½ inch) in width
1 sweet red pepper (capsicum), sliced
1 sweet green pepper (capsicum), chopped chunky
1 garlic clove, finely minced
1 onion, finely chopped
1 tbsp tomato purée
1 tbsp dried thyme
2 tsp paprika
1 tsp chilli powder
2 tsp freshly ground black pepper
115 g (4 oz) butter
50 ml (2 fl oz / 3 tbsp) olive oil
2 tbsp flour
450 ml (15 fl oz / ¾ pt) beef stock
75 ml (3 fl oz / 4 tbsp) dark rum
1 whole and intact Scotch bonnet pepper
salt to taste

Cooking instructions

1. In a heavy duty frying pan, fry the beef a small amount at a time until brown. Set aside in a bowl.

2. Heat gently in a saucepan the olive oil and butter. When the butter has melted add flour, turn the heat up a little, stir continuously to make a golden brown roux. As it reaches the desired colour, add immediately the chopped onions, garlic, sweet red pepper, stirring to mix well before adding the beef, black pepper, tomato purée, chilli powder, paprika and dried thyme.

3. Pour in the stock and rum, stirring well. Bring to the boil, then drop in the whole Scotch bonnet pepper, lower the heat and simmer for 1½ hours or until beef is tender.

4. Add the chunky-chopped, green sweet pepper and cook for another 5-7 minutes. If you wish to have a runny Creole Beef, add a little hot water. Taste and adjust seasoning. Serve with any root vegetable or pasta.

JI BEEF PELAU

very popular dish in Trinidad. Muslim East Indian in origin, its name derives Urdu, **pilao** or **puloa**, meaning rice. The type of pelau is distinguished by the name of the other main ingredient cooked with it, such as chicken or vegetables. Serves 6.

Ingredients

1 kg (2¼ lb) chuck beef or any cut suitable for stewing or braising
lemon or lime water for washing meat (see Miscellany)
1 large onion, finely chopped
2 garlic cloves, finely minced
2 carrots, coarsely chopped
1 green pepper (capsicum), finely chopped
2 tbsp chopped flat leaf parsley
1 whole and intact Scotch bonnet pepper
4 tbsp corn oil or sunflower oil
2 tbsp brown sugar
450 g (1 lb) long grain rice, thoroughly washed
575 ml (20 fl oz / 1 pt) beef stock

For marinade

1 inch cinnamon stick, 1 tsp coarse sea salt, 7 cloves and 2 tsp black pepper
  dry roasted and crushed in a mortar and pestle.
Add 1 tbsp chopped chives, ¼ of a Scotch bonnet pepper (chopped), 2
  garlic cloves, 1 tbsp thyme and crush into a paste.
Pour onto the paste 150 ml (5 fl oz / ¼ pt) of dark rum and 1 tbsp corn oil
  or sunflower oil. Mix well. The marinade paste is now ready to be rubbed
  into the beef.

Cooking instructions

1. Briefly wash the beef in lime or lemon water, then cut it into pieces, using 1½ inches (4 cm) as a guide. Rub the marinade into the beef and set it aside to marinate for at least 1 hour, or preferably overnight.

2. In a heavy-duty saucepan, heat 2 tbsp corn oil or sunflower oil until very hot then add the brown sugar. When the sugar begins to caramelise add the beef and stir vigorously to cover the pieces with caramelised sugar. Turn the heat down a fraction, cover the saucepan and cook for 2-3 minutes before pouring in the stock. Bring to the boil, drop in the

whole and intact Scotch bonnet pepper, lower the heat and simmer for 1½-2 hours. It is important to lift out intact the Scotch bonnet pepper after 1 hour.

3. When the beef is tender, remove it from the saucepan into a bowl. Add hot water to the reduced beef liquor to make 800 ml (40 fl oz / 2 pt) of stock. Pass the stock through a sieve, taste and adjust seasoning; set it aside.

4. In a clean saucepan, fry chopped onion and garlic in 2 tbsp of oil. When the onion pieces begin to be translucent, stir in the rice and cook for 1 minute before adding the carrots and beef stock. Cook gently on very low heat. When the rice has absorbed most of the stock, add the beef, chopped green pepper and parsley. Cover, cook for another 10 minutes or until all liquid is absorbed. The pelau is ready to be served.

HURRY-HURRY CORNED BEEF WITH HERB-BUTTER RICE

Serves 4

Ingredients

2 tins of corned beef
1 large onion, finely chopped
1 red pepper (capsicum), coarsely chopped
1 green pepper (capsicum), diced
1 tin of chopped tomatoes
2 celery stalks, de-strung and finely chopped (save leaves for garnishing)
½ tsp finely minced Scotch bonnet pepper (optional)
1 plump garlic clove, finely minced
1 tsp dried thyme
3 tbsp extra virgin olive oil
150 ml (5 fl oz / ¼ pt) beef stock
225 g (8 oz) long grain rice

For herb butter

58 g (2 oz) unsalted butter
2 tbsp finely chopped basil (or any other herb of your choosing)
½ tsp ground cumin
1 tsp freshly ground black pepper
½ tsp sea salt

Cooking instructions

Make the herb butter beforehand and store it in the refrigerator. To make the herb butter, beat the butter until soft, then add the chopped basil, black pepper, cumin and salt. Blend well and roll it on greaseproof paper into a sausage shape. Twist both ends of the greaseproof paper and set aside in the refrigerator.

1. In a deep, heavy-duty frying pan, fry onion and garlic in 3 tbsp olive oil. When the pieces of chopped onion are translucent and slightly brown around the edges, add red pepper, tomatoes, celery, dried thyme and the minced Scotch bonnet pepper. Stir and cook for 5 minutes, then add beef stock; lower heat and simmer.

2. Cut corned beef into large chunky pieces and add them, with the diced green pepper, to the simmering sauce. Stir very gently so that the chunky pieces do not break up. Continue the simmering so that the corned beef is heated through.

3. Wash and cook rice in 1.1 litre (40 fl oz / 2 pt) of water. When the rice is cooked, drain it through a sieve. Return the rice to the saucepan and add 2 tbsp of herb butter. Stir to integrate the herb butter with the rice. Serve immediately with the corned beef.

BEEF BARE-BACK

Serves 4-6

Ingredients

1 kg (2¼ lb) beef, shin or leg, silverside
lemon water for washing (see Miscellany), plus the juice of 1 lemon
2 plump garlic cloves, bruised
1 bay leaf
1 sprig thyme
225 g (8 oz) shell pasta
1 medium-sized red onion
115 g (4 oz) baby spinach or rocket
225 g (8 oz) tomatoes
2 tbsp chopped basil
1 whole, intact green Scotch bonnet pepper
2 tsp freshly ground black pepper
150 ml (5 fl oz / ¼ pt) white rum
4 tbsp extra virgin olive oil
450 ml (15 fl oz / ¾ pt) water
salt to taste

Cooking instructions

1. Briefly wash the beef in lemon water, rinse and chop into 1½ inch (4 cm) cubes.

2. Pour 450 ml (15 fl oz/¾ pt) water into a saucepan; set it on high heat. Add white rum, garlic, bay leaf, thyme, the juice of 1 lemon, salt and the beef. Cook at a rolling boil for 5 minutes, lower the heat, and with saucepan lid off, reduce the cooking to a simmer. Partially cover the saucepan, drop in the Scotch bonnet pepper and cook for 1½-2 hours, or until beef is tender. Very carefully remove the Scotch bonnet pepper without rupturing it.

3. Wash baby spinach or rocket; slice the red onion very thinly. Remove the boiled beef from its liquor with a slotted spoon into a large serving dish; and while it is hot, add the spinach or rocket, thinly sliced red onion, black pepper, olive oil, salt if needed, and toss together. Keep warm.

4. Pass the beef liquor through a sieve into another saucepan. Add 175 ml (6 fl oz) water to the liquor. Bring it to the boil, add the pasta and cook to al dente. The cooking of the pasta should absorb most of the liquor. Add the de-seeded quartered tomatoes, basil, and olive oil; mix together. Serve with the beef.

MAMMIE BEEF STEW
Serves 4-6

Ingredients

1 kg (2¼ lb) stewing steak (skirt, chuck or brisket)
lime or lemon water for washing (see Miscellany)
1 tbsp corn oil
1 tbsp brown sugar
170 g (6 oz) carrot, sliced
225 g (8 oz) potato, cut into 1½ inch (4 cm) dice
1 large onion, chopped
2 garlic cloves, finely minced
300 ml (10 fl oz / ½ pt) beef or vegetable stock
300 ml (10 fl oz / ½ pt) brown beer
1 sprig thyme
1 whole and intact Scotch bonnet pepper
salt and freshly ground black pepper to taste

For marinade

1 chopped garlic clove
2 tbsp grated green paw-paw (papaya) skin
1 tbsp chopped chives
150 ml (5 fl oz / ¼ pt) rum
2 tsp freshly ground black pepper, and salt to taste

Cooking instructions

1. Briefly wash beef in lime or lemon water; pat dry and cut into pieces, using 1½ inches (4 cm) as a guide.

2. Using a food processor or mortar and pestle, combine the marinade ingredients to make a paste. Rub into the beef and set aside for at least 1 hour or, preferably, overnight.

3. In a heavy-duty saucepan or cast iron pot, heat the corn oil. When it is very hot, add sugar, which will soon begin to caramelise. At this point, add the beef, stirring vigorously to coat the pieces with caramelised sugar. Cover and reduce heat a little. The beef will spring its own juices. When the juices have almost dried up, stir in the onion, minced garlic and a little more oil if needed. Cook until the onion is soft and translucent. Add the stock, beer, sprig of thyme and the whole, intact Scotch bonnet pepper; bring to the boil, lower heat and simmer for 1 hour.

4. Carefully remove, without rupturing, the Scotch bonnet pepper. Taste and adjust the seasoning if necessary. Add the potatoes and carrots. Cook for another ½ hour. Serve with boiled rice and kidney beans.

PEPPER YUH-TAIL FRYING STEAK

Both a threat to errant small boys, and another way of saying, *ah go use a lot a pepper*. In this recipe the caramelised sugar with its high temperature seals the meat rapidly and adds a sweetish flavour. Serves 2

Ingredients

225 g (8 oz) rump or sirloin steak
lime water for washing (see Miscellany)
I severely bruised plump garlic clove
50 ml (2 fl oz/3 tbsp) corn or groundnut oil
2 tbsp brown cane sugar
2 tbsp coarsely ground black pepper
salt to taste

Cooking instructions

1. Rinse steak in lime water. Pat dry with kitchen paper towels.

2. Spread I tbsp of ground black pepper and a sprinkling of flaked sea salt on a clean chopping board. Rub both sides of the steak with crushed garlic. Lay the steak in the black pepper. Cover the steak with cling film and beat it with a meat mallet. Give the same treatment to the other side.

3. Heat the oil in a heavy-duty skillet until it is very hot. Sprinkle the sugar into the hot oil. When it begins to caramelise, carefully lay the beaten steak onto the bubbling sugar for 2 seconds, turn the steak on to the other side and press flat with a steak bat or spatula. Cook the steak to your liking: rare, medium or well-done. Serve immediately with a tomato salad.

MINCED BEEF WITH RED CABBAGE
Serves 4-6

Ingredients

675 g (1½ lb) minced beef
1 shredded red cabbage
1 large onion, finely chopped
3 garlic cloves, finely minced
2 celery stalks, de-strung and finely chopped
3 tbsp pickled red cabbage
1 tbsp tomato purée
1 tbsp red wine vinegar
1 tbsp caster sugar
1 tsp finely minced, de-seeded Scotch bonnet pepper
1 sprig of thyme
1 tbsp chopped flat leaf parsley
3 tbsp plain flour
75 ml (3 fl oz/4 tbsp) virgin olive oil
1 tbsp butter
575 ml (20 fl oz/1 pt) light vegetable stock
1 tsp freshly ground black pepper
sea salt to taste

Cooking instructions

1. In a large saucepan with a tight lid, heat the olive oil and butter. Remove the saucepan from the heat and stir in the flour vigorously to make a smooth mixture. Return the saucepan to the heat and continue to stir until the mixture becomes a light golden roux.

2. Add the onions, garlic and celery. Stir and cook until the onion begins to show translucency. Put in the minced beef with the tomato purée, caster sugar, red wine vinegar, pickled red cabbage and Scotch bonnet pepper. Add a little more olive oil if necessary and stir to combine the ingredients. Cook for another 3-5 minutes before adding the vegetable stock. Season with black pepper and salt to taste. Drop in the sprig of thyme; cover and simmer for 1½ hours.

3. Taste to make sure the beef is tender, then add the shredded red cabbage, the chopped parsley and continue cooking for 10-15 minutes. Serve immediately with fried plantain and boiled rice.

BEEF SAGABOY

A sagaboy was the old-time term for a flashy dresser, as dandy as the beef in this recipe. Serves 6.

Ingredients

1 kg (2¼ lb) braising steak (skirt or chuck from a butcher's shop), cut into strips
1 tsp ground cinnamon
1 tbsp freshly ground black pepper
2 tsp paprika powder
5 cloves
1 tsp ground ginger
2 garlic cloves, finely chopped
1 large onion, coarsely chopped
1 red pepper (capsicum), chunkily chopped
1 green pepper (capsicum), chunkily chopped
½ Scotch bonnet pepper, de-seeded and finely chopped (optional)
1 tsp grated root ginger
1 tbsp molasses
3 tbsp corn oil
450 ml (15 fl oz / ¾ pt) vegetable stock
150 ml (5 fl oz / ¼ pt) Caribbean rum
1 tsp chopped rosemary
1 sprig of thyme
4 tbsp natural yoghurt
salt to taste

Cooking instructions

1. Put into a small glass bowl the cinnamon, ground black pepper, paprika and ground ginger; mix into a homogenous whole, a condition easily judged by the evenness of the colour in the mixture.

2. In another bowl, put together the grated root ginger, chopped garlic, finely chopped Scotch bonnet pepper (if using) and yoghurt. Add the powdered ingredients, mix thoroughly into a marinade; rub it into the strips of beef and put aside to marinate for at least 30 minutes to 1 hour.

3. In a large saucepan with a lid, heat the corn oil until quite hot; fry the chopped onion until it turns light brown and translucent. Add the beef, stirring to integrate it well with the onions. At this point, put in the molasses, stir and cook for 2 minutes before adding the chopped red pepper.

4. Add the rum, vegetable stock, cloves, rosemary and the sprig of thyme. Taste for seasoning and adjust if necessary. Cover and reduce heat to cook beef until tender. Add the chopped green pepper and cook for a further 3 minutes. Serve with pasta, rice or any root vegetable you like.

CURRIED BEEF
Serves 4-6

Ingredients

1 kg (2¼ lb) stewing steak, washed and cut into 1 inch (2½ cm) cubes
2 large onions, chopped
3 plump garlic cloves
2 tsp black peppercorns
2 tbsp cumin seeds
1 tbsp coriander seeds
7 cloves
5 green cardamoms
1½ inch (3½ cm) cinnamon bark
1 tbsp turmeric powder
1 tbsp paprika powder
1 tsp dried ginger powder
1 tbsp tomato purée
1 green sweet pepper (capsicum), chopped coarsely
1 red sweet pepper (capsicum), finely chopped
1 hot red chilli, de-seeded and finely chopped
4 tbsp corn or sunflower oil
850 ml (30 fl oz / 1½ pt) water
salt

Cooking instructions

1. Dry-roast in a small frying pan the peppercorns, cumin seeds, coriander seeds, cloves, cardamoms and cinnamon bark. When the aroma of these spices rises to titillate the nostrils, remove from the heat, transfer to a mortar and crush to a powder with the pestle. Mix in the dry ginger, turmeric and paprika. Add the chilli, garlic and 2 tsp sea salt. Continue to crush to a pulp. Stir into the pulp 1 tbsp oil to complete the curry paste.

2. Rub half of the curry paste into the beef cubes and set aside to marinate for at least an hour, preferably overnight.

3. In a large cast iron pot or saucepan with lid, heat 3 tbsp of oil and fry the onions until they become brown and translucent. Add beef, the rest of the curry paste and continue to cook while stirring to ensure that the beef and curry paste are well integrated. Next, introduce to the mix the red sweet pepper and tomato purée, stir and cook for 5-10 minutes. Add water, cover, lower the heat and simmer until tender.

4. When the beef is tender, turn up the heat to reduce the liquid to a thick sauce; add the sweet green pepper and cook for another 3 minutes. Taste for salt, adjust if needed and serve immediately with plain boiled rice.

RABBIT LA KATANY

'La Katany' is the name of a chalet in Ramberviller, France where I was taught to cook rabbit using this recipe.

Serves 4-6.

Ingredients

I whole rabbit, jointed, washed in lemon
   water (see Miscellany), and patted dry
3 tbsp Dijon mustard
6 cloves of garlic, crushed
3 shallots, peeled and halved
2 tsp coarsely ground black pepper
5 grains of allspice, crushed
I inch piece of cinnamon stick
½ red chilli, finely minced
I sprig of rosemary or ½ tbsp dried rosemary
I sprig of thyme or I tsp dried thyme
3 tbsp olive oil
300 ml (10 fl oz / ½ pt) vegetable stock or chicken stock
300 ml (10 fl oz / ½ pt) dry white wine
I tbsp chopped fresh tarragon or I tsp dried tarragon
salt to taste

Cooking instructions

1. Smother the rabbit pieces with the mustard, black pepper and garlic. Set aside to marinate for at least I hour.

2. Heat the olive oil in a large cast iron pot or a heavy-bottomed saucepan with a lid until quite hot. Add the rabbit and fry, turning it on all sides until light brown.

3. Add the shallots, allspice, red chilli and cinnamon; stir to integrate all these ingredients and cook on reduced heat for 10-15 minutes with pot covered and stirring from time to time.

4. Add stock, white wine, thyme, tarragon and rosemary. Increase the heat to bring liquid to the boil; then, reduce heat and simmer for 30-45 minutes or until rabbit is tender. If a thick sauce is required, remove rabbit, turn up the heat to boil the sauce rapidly to reduce to the desired thickness; or alternatively, mix I tsp corn flour with a little water and add to the sauce. Cook for a further 5 minutes, stirring until it thickens. Adjust seasoning if needed. Serve the rabbit in its sauce with boiled potatoes or your favourite pasta.

BRER RABBIT STEW
Serves 6

Ingredients

1 whole rabbit, jointed, washed in lemon water and patted dry
4 rashers of smoked streaky bacon, coarsely chopped
1 large onion, chunkily chopped
2 garlic cloves, coarsely chopped
2 large carrots, thickly sliced
3 medium-sized potatoes, peeled and cut into quarters
2 celery sticks, de-strung and sliced
2 sweet red peppers (capsicums), chunkily chopped
1 tsp dried tarragon
1 tsp dried thyme
1 tbsp chopped coriander
1 whole and intact Scotch bonnet pepper
2 tsp coarsely ground black pepper
1 tsp mixed spice
40 ml (2 tbsp) extra virgin olive oil
28 g (1 oz) butter
1 tbsp plain flour
1 litre (35 fl oz / 1¾ pt) vegetable stock
salt to taste

Cooking instructions

1. Heat oil in a large cast iron pot or thick-bottomed saucepan with lid until hot. Add the butter; and when the butter is melted, seal the jointed rabbit by frying it in the hot oil and butter.

2. When the meat is brown on all sides, add the onion and fry until it becomes brown and translucent; add the garlic, bacon, mixed spice, black pepper. Stir to bring all the ingredients together and fry for 2 minutes before adding the flour. Stir to integrate it with the bacon and spices.

3. Add the carrots, potatoes, sweet red peppers and celery. Stir and cook the vegetables for 1 or 2 minutes, then add the stock while continuing to stir. Bring to the boil, lower heat, add the whole and intact Scotch bonnet pepper, the tarragon and thyme; simmer for 30-45 minutes, or until meat is tender. Remove the Scotch bonnet pepper and sprinkle in the chopped coriander. If a thick stew is desired, turn up the heat to medium and cook for a further 5-10 minutes uncovered. Taste and adjust seasoning if needed. Serve while still hot.

MOROCCAN-INSPIRED LAMB
Serves 4-6

Ingredients

I lamb shoulder about I kg (2¼ lb), washed in lemon water (see Miscellany), rinsed, patted dry and chopped into chunks, including bone. If bought at a traditional butcher, a friendly request for it to be chopped as required for this recipe would be useful.

For marinade

I tbsp of coarsely ground black pepper, 2 tsp ground cinnamon, 3 bruised cloves, 50 ml (2 fl oz/3 tbsp) dark rum, juice of ½ a lemon, salt to taste and I tbsp olive oil

Other ingredients

2 large onions, coarsely chopped
3 plump garlic cloves, finely minced
I tbsp ground cumin
I tsp paprika
I tsp chilli powder
I tbsp ground coriander
2 star anise
2 inch (5 cm) piece of cinnamon stick
5 whole green chillies (optional)
4 large tomatoes, skinned, de-seeded and chopped; or I tin chopped tomatoes
115 g (4 oz) sultanas
3 large carrots, peeled and cut into wedges
2 red peppers (capsicum), each chopped into 6 pieces
I tbsp flat leaf parsley, chopped
I tbsp coarsely chopped coriander
I tbsp chopped fresh mint
150 ml (¼ pt) freshly squeezed orange juice
75 ml (3 fl oz/4 tbsp) extra virgin olive oil
400 ml (14 fl oz/ ⅔ pt) water or light vegetable stock

Cooking instructions

1. Combine the ingredients for the marinade. Rub the mixture into the lamb and put aside to marinate for at least 3 hours; overnight is a better option.

2. In a very large tajine set on a barbecue fire (or a large, thick-bottomed saucepan with a lid, on the cooker, set on high heat), fry the onions, stirring from time to time until they are translucent and brown. Add ground cumin, ground coriander, paprika, chilli powder, cinnamon stick and star anise; fry for about 30 seconds, or until spices give off their aroma. Add garlic and lamb, stirring vigorously to integrate the chunks of lamb with the other ingredients. Cook for 15 minutes.

3. Stir in the tomatoes and orange juice. Add the stock; taste for salt, bring to the boil and lower heat. Cover and simmer for 1-1½ hours.

4. Add carrots, sultanas, red peppers, parsley and whole green chillies (if being used). Cook for a further 20 minutes. Test for seasoning and tenderness of lamb. Remove from the heat and sprinkle in the coarsely chopped mint and coriander, give it a stir. Let it rest for 3 minutes before serving with couscous.

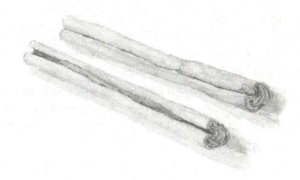

COCOTTE LAMB

'Cocotte' is the French word for casserole and in Trinidad it is an expression of endearment. I love this dish.

Serves 4.

Ingredients

675 g (1½ lb) breast or leg of lamb, rinsed in lemon water (see Miscellany) and cut into small chunks

125 ml (7 tbsp) natural yoghurt (50 ml/3 tbsp for marinade; 75 ml/4 tbsp to be mixed with stock)

2 cloves of garlic, finely minced

2 tsp freshly ground black pepper

1 tbsp Dijon mustard

1 onion, finely chopped

½ green chilli, de-seeded and coarsely chopped

2 tbsp extra virgin olive oil

1 tsp dried thyme

1 tsp dried oregano

1 sprig of fresh mint

300 ml (10 fl oz/½ pt) cold chicken stock

salt to taste

Cooking instructions

1. Combine 3 tbsp yoghurt, garlic, salt, black pepper and mustard. Add the lamb to it and set aside to marinate for 1-3 hours.

2. On moderate heat, sauté onion in olive oil in a thick-based saucepan. When the finely chopped onion is soft and translucent, add the lamb, chilli, thyme and oregano. Cook for 20 minutes stirring from time to time to prevent sticking.

3. Combine the cold stock and remaining 4 tbsp yoghurt, then add to the lamb. Taste for salt. Lower heat, add sprig of mint, cover and simmer gently for 1-1½ hours. Serve with sticky herb rice.

SATURDAY STEWED LAMB
Serves 4-6

Ingredients

1 kg (2¼ lb) lamb shoulder, washed in lime water (see Miscellany),
   rinsed and cut into chunks
2 large onions, coarsely chopped
3 garlic cloves, finely minced
2 large carrots, peeled and cut into small wedges
1 Scotch bonnet pepper
225 g (8 oz) potatoes, peeled, washed and cut into wedges
170 g (6 oz) macaroni
2 tsp finely ground black peppercorns
½ tsp freshly grated nutmeg
800 ml (28 fl oz) vegetable stock
1 bay leaf
1 sprig thyme
2 tsp caster sugar
salt to taste
3 tbsp olive oil
28 g (1 oz) butter
1 tbsp plain white flour

Cooking instructions

1. In a large saucepan with a thick bottom, melt on moderate heat the butter in hot olive oil. Add flour and stir continuously to form a golden roux.
2. Add onions and garlic; sauté for 5 minutes or until onions become translucent. Add the lamb, sugar, black pepper; stir well to integrate ingredients then add stock. Bring to the boil, lower heat; add bay leaf and Scotch bonnet pepper whole and intact, simmer for 1½ hours.
3. Add carrots and potatoes. Carefully remove the Scotch bonnet pepper without rupturing it. Add salt and cook for another 15 minutes. Add macaroni, thyme and nutmeg; cook for another 10 minutes. Taste and adjust seasoning if needed. Serve immediately.

RUM LAMB SHANK
Serves 1-2

Ingredients

2 lamb shanks, washed in lime or lemon water (see Miscellany), rinsed
  and patted dry
I medium-sized onion, finely sliced
6 garlic cloves in their skins
I tsp whole black peppercorns
2 tsp sea salt
I inch (2½ cm) piece of cinnamon stick
I sprig rosemary
I sprig thyme
75 ml (3 fl oz/4 tbsp) Trinidad rum
2 dashes Angostura bitters
300 ml (10 fl oz/½ pt) vegetable stock
50 ml (2 fl oz/3 tbsp) single cream (optional)
50 ml (2 fl oz/3 tbsp) groundnut or corn oil

Cooking instructions

1. Heat oil in an oven-proof casserole until quite hot. Brown the lamb
   shanks on all sides along with black peppercorns and the piece of cinnamon
   stick. When almost brown on all sides add onions and garlic. Continue
   frying until lamb is fully brown.

2. Add rum, 2 dashes of Angostura bitters, stock, rosemary and thyme;
   cover tightly and bring to the boil. Reduce heat and simmer for 10 minutes.
   Turn the shanks so that their whole surface can receive the benefit of
   the rum and stock.

3. Put the casserole in the oven pre-heated at 180°C/350°F/gas mark 4.
   Cook for 1-1½ hours, or until tender.

4. Remove casserole from the oven and onto the cooker. Transfer the
   shanks to a covered dish and keep warm in the oven, turned off.

5. Add to the casserole 250 ml (8 fl oz/ ⅓ pt) hot water; increase the
   heat to bring the liquor to a rapid boil. Stir with a wooden spoon, while
   crushing the cooked garlic against the sides of the casserole.

6. Pass the contents of the casserole through a sieve into a serving bowl,
   pushing with the wooden spoon most of the onions and garlic through
   the mesh. This process thickens the sauce. Taste and adjust the seasoning
   if needed. Add cream, if it is being used. Serve the shanks with the
   sauce poured over it.

LAMB-STUFFED GREEN PEPPERS
Serves 4

Ingredients

450 g (1 lb) lamb leg, rinsed in lime or lemon water (see Miscellany) and
    cut into 1 inch (2½ cm) cubes
4 green sweet peppers (capsicum), hollowed out from the stalk end for
    stuffing
3 carrots, washed, peeled and chunkily chopped
2 rashers of smoked bacon (dry-cured, if possible), coarsely chopped
1 onion, sliced
2 garlic cloves, coarsely chopped
1 green chilli, de-seeded and coarsely chopped
1 tbsp chopped coriander
1 tsp thyme
1 tsp ground cumin
1 tsp turmeric powder
2 tsp mustard seeds
1 tsp freshly ground black pepper
300 ml (10 fl oz/½ pt) light vegetable stock
3 tbsp extra virgin olive oil for frying
salt to taste

Cooking instructions

1. Put through a meat mincer or food processor the following ingredients:
lamb, sliced onion, garlic, chopped rashers of bacon and chopped green
chilli.

2. Put into a mixing bowl. Add salt, thyme, chopped coriander and combine,
using the ideal tool for this task, your hands.

3. Heat 3 tbsp olive oil in a cast iron pot or a saucepan with a thick base
on moderate heat. Add cumin, turmeric, black pepper and mustard
seeds. Fry for 30 seconds in the hot oil before adding the minced lamb.
Stir vigorously to integrate the lamb with the fried spices. Cook for 10
minutes, stirring from time to time.

4. Add stock and bring to the boil; lower heat and simmer until lamb is
tender and most of the liquid gone. This should take 30-45 minutes.
Remove from heat and leave to rest for 10 minutes. Stuff the green
peppers with the lamb and set aside.

5. Heat 2 tbsp olive oil in a frying pan. Add the carrots, fry for 5 minutes
then empty into an oven-proof casserole. Arrange the 4 stuffed peppers

upright among the carrots. Drizzle a generous amount of olive oil on the peppers and carrots, put into a pre-heated oven and bake at 205°C/ 400°F/gas mark 6 for 20-30 minutes. Serve with couscous and a spicy tomato sauce.

LAMB WITH SPINACH
Serves 4-6

Ingredients

1 kg (2¼ lb) lamb leg, rinsed in lime or lemon water (see Miscellany),
  patted dry and cut into 1 inch (2½ cm) cubes
250 g (½ lb) spinach
2 large onions, finely chopped
3 garlic cloves, finely minced
½ inch (1¼ cm) piece of root ginger, grated
2 tsp tomato purée
2 tsp mustard seeds
1 tbsp ground cumin
1 tsp coarsely ground black pepper
1 tsp lemon zest
1 whole and intact Scotch bonnet pepper
400 ml (14 fl oz) light vegetable stock
3 tbsp corn oil
salt to taste

Cooking instructions

1. Wash spinach thoroughly; if bought from an organic greengrocer or taken from your own kitchen garden, include a little salt in the water for the first wash. Pour boiling water on the spinach, leave for 30 seconds, pass through a strainer or colander and immediately run the cold tap through it. Set aside to drain.

2. In a saucepan with a thick base, fry black pepper, ground cumin and mustard seeds for 30 seconds on moderate heat, while stirring. Add onions, ginger and garlic. When the onions have become translucent and light brown, add the lamb, tomato purée and salt to taste. Stir well to integrate all the ingredients. Cook for 3-5 minutes.

3. Add light vegetable stock. Bring to the boil, lower heat, add Scotch bonnet pepper and simmer for 1½-2 hours. Remove the Scotch bonnet pepper very carefully. Fold the wilted spinach and the lemon zest into the lamb and cook for a further 3-5 minutes before serving with plain boiled rice.

BROWN LAMB

Serves 4

Ingredients

1 kg (2¼ lb) lamb leg, cut into medium chunks and marinated for at least
    3 hours

For marinade

1 finely chopped onion; 3 garlic cloves, finely minced; 1 tbsp chopped thyme;
1 tbsp chopped chives; 1 tsp freshly ground black pepper; ½ Scotch bonnet
pepper, de-seeded and finely minced; 3 tbsp rum; ½ tsp madras curry powder;
salt to taste. All ingredients thoroughly mixed.

Other ingredients

2 tbsp brown cane sugar
3 tbsp sunflower oil or corn oil
400 ml (14 fl oz/ ⅔ pt) vegetable stock

Cooking instructions

1. In a cast iron pot with lid or a thick-bottomed saucepan with lid, heat
   the oil until very hot. Add the sugar; and when it bubbles like caramel,
   add the marinated lamb and stir vigorously to cover all the chunks of
   lamb with the caramelised sugar.

2. Add vegetable stock, stir, cover, reduce heat and simmer for 1½ hours.
   Test for seasoning, adjust if needed. Also test for tenderness and if cooked,
   uncover the saucepan, raise the heat to reduce almost all the liquid.
   Serve with freshly baked bread or johnnie bake.

When my grandmother cooked meat in this way, it was sometimes kept
covered in a cool storage cabinet, which we called a 'safe', for a few days
during which time, portions of it were used as part of quick-cooked meals.

A TRINI'S CURRIED LAMB'S KIDNEYS

Serves 4-6

Ingredients

10-12 lamb's kidneys
lemon water for rinsing (see Miscellany)
1 large onion, finely chopped
3 garlic cloves, finely minced
2 red sweet peppers (capsicum), chunkily cut
1 green sweet pepper, cut into ½-inch (1 cm) squares
1 bay leaf
3 tbsp sunflower oil or corn oil
300 ml (10 fl oz/½ pt) chicken stock
salt to taste

For marinade

4 tbsp freshly squeezed lime juice
2 tbsp dark rum
1 tsp grated root ginger
1 tsp finely minced Scotch bonnet pepper
2 tsp sea salt

For curry paste

½ tsp black peppercorns
½ tsp mustard seeds
1 tbsp coriander seeds
1 tsp cumin seeds
1 inch (2½ cm) cinnamon stick
3 cloves
1 tsp turmeric powder
1 tsp masala
50 ml (2 fl oz/3 tbsp) water

Cooking instructions

1. Remove the skin from the kidneys. Cut them in half and with a pair of scissors, snip away the gristle. Rinse in lemon water, pat dry.
2. Combine the ingredients for the marinade. Add the kidneys, mix well into the marinade and set aside for 1 hour.

3. In a frying pan, dry-fry the ingredients for the curry paste, with the exception of the turmeric and masala. When the spices begin to release their aroma, transfer them to a mortar and pound them to a powder. Add the masala, turmeric and the water, stir into a curry paste.

4. In a cast iron pot or saucepan with a thick base, heat the oil until hot. Add the onions and fry until light brown. Add garlic and fry for 30 seconds. Stir in the curry paste and cook for one minute before adding the kidneys. Mix them well into the curry paste.

5. Add the sweet red peppers, cover the pot, lower the heat to medium and cook for 5-10 minutes, stirring frequently.

6. Add the stock and bay leaf; increase the heat to bring to the boil, then lower the heat to its minimum. Simmer gently for 1½ hours, or until tender. Add the green sweet pepper 3 minutes before turning the heat off to serve.

CURRIED GOAT

Serves 4-6

This recipe is as good also for mutton, venison or any other wild game whose muscular, free existence has sweetened its flesh.

Ingredients

1 kg (2¼ lb) goat meat, cut into chunks, preferably with the bone
lime or lemon water for washing (see Miscellany)
2 large onions, finely chopped
1 clove garlic, finely minced
1 bay leaf
1 whole and intact Scotch bonnet pepper
7 green cardamoms, husked for their seeds
1 inch (2½ cm) cinnamon stick
1 tbsp cumin seeds
2 tsp curry powder
2 tsp black peppercorns
1 generous tbsp gram flour
28 g (1 oz) butter
3 tbsp corn oil or sunflower oil
250 ml (8 fl oz/ ⅓ pt) light vegetable stock
salt to taste

For marinade

1 tsp black peppercorns
3 cloves
2 tsp allspice
3 tsp curry powder
2 tsp coarse salt
½ Scotch bonnet pepper, de-seeded
2 tsp grated ginger
2 garlic cloves
1 tbsp sunflower or corn oil
50 ml (2 fl oz/3 tbsp) white rum

Cooking instructions

1. Prepare the marinade: dry fry in a small frying pan: peppercorns, cloves, allspice and coarse salt. When the spices begin to release their aroma, remove from the heat and grind them to a powder with a mortar and

pestle. Add the grated ginger, Scotch bonnet pepper, garlic and curry powder. Pound to a paste, then stir in the oil and rum.

2. Wash the meat in lime or lemon water; rinse and drain. Put it into a large mixing bowl, add the marinade paste. Rub it well into the meat, cover and leave it to marinate for about 24 hours, or overnight at least.

3. Heat the oil in a cast iron pot, or saucepan with a thick base, until hot. Add the butter and when it melts add the cumin seeds; fry for 3 seconds before adding the onions. Cook them until brown. Add the garlic, peppercorns, cardamom seeds and cinnamon stick. Continue frying for 1 minute and sprinkle in the gram flour, stirring well to mix it into the other ingredients. Add the curry powder and a little more oil if dry.

4. Stir in the marinated meat to integrate it well with the other ingredients. Put the lid on, lower to medium heat and continue to cook for 5-10 minutes, stirring frequently.

5. Pour in the vegetable stock, bring to the boil, drop in the bay leaf and the whole and intact Scotch bonnet pepper, lower heat to the minimum and simmer gently for 1½ hours or until meat is tender. Carefully remove the Scotch bonnet pepper. Stir well before serving. It is delicious with roti or plain boiled rice. This curried goat gets better aged 1-2 days in the refrigerator, that is, if you can wait that long.

STEWED PORK WITH BUTTER BEANS
Serves 4

Ingredients

1 kg (2¼ lb) belly pork, put into boiling salted water on high heat for 5
    minutes, drained in a colander and rinsed under a running cold tap,
    then cut into 1½ inch (4 cm) pieces
225 (8 oz) dried butter beans, soaked overnight and cooked in unsalted
    water until soft and still whole
1 large onion, coarsely chopped
1 plump garlic clove, finely minced
115 g (4 oz) smoked bacon, coarsely chopped
1 whole and intact Scotch bonnet pepper
1 tsp caster sugar
1 tsp turmeric powder
1 tsp tomato purée
400 ml (14 fl oz) vegetable stock
2 tbsp extra virgin olive oil
1 bouquet garni of sage, rosemary, thyme and bay leaf
salt to taste

For marinade

2 tbsp freshly squeezed lime juice
2 tsp ground ginger
1 tbsp chopped sage
1 tbsp chopped chives
1 tbsp freshly ground black pepper
1 plump garlic clove, finely minced
1 tbsp white rum (optional)
salt to taste

Cooking instructions

1. Trim away some of the pork fat from under the skin. Combine all the
    ingredients to make the marinade, add the pork to it, mixing well with
    your hands to ensure that all the pieces come into contact with the
    marinade. Set aside to marinate for at least 3 hours.
2. Heat the olive oil in a deep thick-bottomed frying pan with a lid, add
    onions and fry until they become translucent. Add garlic, bacon and
    turmeric powder. Stir and cook for 5 minutes before adding the marinated

pork; then mix in the tomato purée and sugar. Cook for 10 minutes, stirring from time to time.

3. Add the stock, the whole, intact Scotch bonnet pepper and bouquet garni. Bring to the boil, lower heat and simmer gently for 1½-2 hours, or until pork is tender. Remove the Scotch bonnet pepper, add the butter beans. Stir them gently into the stew. Taste and adjust seasoning if needed. Serve with boiled sweet potato.

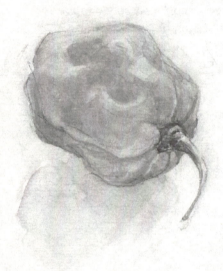

ROAST PORK WITH AN EGO
Serves 4-6

Ingredients

1 kg (2¼ lb) loin pork, rinsed in strong lime water, patted dry
1 tsp mustard powder
1 tbsp sea salt
1 tbsp olive oil
½ Scotch bonnet pepper, finely minced
2 tsp finely chopped sage, or 1 tsp dried sage
2 tsp finely chopped thyme, or 1 tsp dried thyme
1 tsp finely chopped rosemary, or ¼ tsp dried rosemary, finely chopped
2 shallots, finely chopped
1 plump garlic clove, finely minced
1 tsp grated ginger
115 g (4 oz) brown soft sugar
1 tbsp dark rum
1 tsp freshly ground black pepper
1 tbsp plain white flour
75 ml (3 fl oz/4 tbsp) medium dry sherry
150 ml (5 fl oz/¼ pt) pure apple juice

Cooking instructions

1. Mix together the olive oil, salt and mustard powder. Rub this mixture into the skin of the pork. With a very sharp knife make even, deep, parallel cuts, about ¾ inch (2 cm) in width, through the skin and into the fat to just reach the lean meat below.

2. Combine in a small bowl the Scotch bonnet pepper, herbs, shallots, ginger, garlic and a little salt. Rub this mixture deep into the parallel cuts.

3. Put the pork in a roasting tin, cover with kitchen foil, tucking it over the edge of the tin. Roast in a pre-heated oven, 200°C/400°F/gas mark 6, for 40 minutes; then remove the foil covering, reduce the heat to 160°C/325°F/gas mark 3 and continue roasting for 45 minutes, basting frequently. Combine the sugar, rum and black pepper. Pour this mixture over the pork. Roast for 30 minutes more.

4. Remove the pork from the roasting tin, set aside to relax. Spoon out some of the excess fat from the roasting tin if too much. On a moderate heat on the top of the cooker, add to the tin 1 tbsp plain white flour. Stir well to integrate the flour with the remaining fat and protein residue of the pork. Pour in, a little at a time while stirring, the sherry and apple juice to form a roux. Taste and adjust seasoning if needed. The sauce must have a smooth, runny, not-too-thick consistency for easy pouring over the slices of roast pork.

JAMETTE PORK

A bit-ah-hot-stuff: from the name for those whom the colonial authorities and respectable folk regarded as the wild, riotous members of carnival bands; from French 'diametres', outside the bounds. Serves 4-6

Ingredients

1 kg (2¼ lb) pork fillets (tenderloin), washed in lime water and patted dry
20 ml (1 tbsp) dark soy sauce
1 tbsp (15 g/½ oz) muscovado sugar
1 tbsp (15 g/½ oz) grated root ginger
1 tsp sherry vinegar
1 tsp finely minced Scotch bonnet pepper
1 tbsp sesame oil
1 tsp black peppercorns
50 ml (2 fl oz/3 tbsp) peanut oil
450 ml (15 fl oz/¾ pt) chicken stock
50 ml (2 fl oz/3 tbsp) medium dry sherry
3 bruised garlic cloves
1 tsp cornflour
3 green chillies, sliced diagonally into 4 pieces (optional)
3 red chillies, sliced diagonally into 4 pieces

Cooking instructions

1. Mix together in a bowl the soy sauce, grated ginger, sherry vinegar, finely minced Scotch bonnet pepper and sesame oil. Add the pork to it. With your hands, rub the marinade into the pork and set aside to marinate for at least 3 hours or, ideally, overnight.

2. Heat the peanut oil in a cast iron pot with lid, or a flameproof casserole, on medium heat until hot, add the garlic and peppercorns. When the garlic cloves become brown, remove them from the oil with a slotted spoon. Add the sugar. When sugar begins to bubble, add the pork fillets and fry until brown on all sides.

3. Mix the stock with the marinade, pour over the pork, bring to the boil, lower heat to simmer gently for 1½ hours, basting frequently, until tender.

4. Remove the pork from the pot. Pass the liquid which is left in the pot through a sieve. Return this strained sauce to the pot. Add the sherry to it along with the chillies (if being used). Continue cooking a little to reduce the sauce and drive off the alcohol. Taste for seasoning, adjust if needed and stir in the cornflour mixed with 1 tbsp water. Keep stirring as the sauce thickens.

5. Cut the pork fillets diagonally into slices ½ inch (1 cm) thick. Serve with the sherry sauce poured over the pork slices. It goes well with green French beans, roasted parsnips and sweet potatoes.

CUFF-DONG SPARERIBS

So tasty, *yuh cuff it dong in no time*. Serves 4-6

Ingredients

12 pork spareribs
lemon water for washing (see Miscellany)
2 tbsp brown sugar
3 tbsp groundnut oil
1 tbsp ground cinnamon

For marinade

2 tbsp clear honey
2 tbsp freshly squeezed lime juice
Scotch bonnet pepper to your personal taste, finely minced
1 tbsp salt
2 tsp freshly ground black pepper
2 garlic cloves, finely minced
1 tsp sage, finely chopped
1 tsp thyme, finely chopped
50 ml (2 fl oz/3 tbsp) rum
1 tsp Angostura bitters

Cooking instructions

1. Rinse the spareribs in lemon water, pat dry ready for the marinade. Combine all the ingredients to make the marinade, add the spareribs to it. Marinate overnight, or, at least, for 3 hours.

2. In a large cast iron pot, or deep frying pan with a lid and a heavy base, heat the oil until very hot. Add the sugar. When it begins to bubble into caramel, immediately add the spareribs and stir vigorously to ensure that all the spareribs are covered with the caramelised sugar. Cook on high heat for 2 minutes, stirring regularly. Add a little water, about 150 ml (5 fl oz/¼ pt); lower heat and continue cooking, stirring from time to time until the liquid has dried up.

3. Remove the spareribs from the frying pan, put into a baking tin and continue cooking in the oven at 190°C/375°F/gas mark 5 for 20 minutes or until tender. Remove from the oven, dust with the ground cinnamon and set aside to rest for 1-2 minutes before serving.

DOLLS-UP PORK CHOPS

Serves 4

Ingredients

4 pork chops, rinsed in lemon water (see Miscellany), patted dry
2 tbsp coarsely ground black pepper
3 tbsp coarsely chopped unsalted peanuts or mixed nuts
2 garlic cloves
1 small onion, grated
1 tsp tomato purée
¼ Scotch bonnet pepper, finely minced
4 tbsp groundnut oil
50 ml (2 fl oz/3 tbsp) medium dry sherry
150 ml (5 fl oz/¼ pt) chicken stock
75 ml (3 fl oz/4 tbsp) single cream
½ tsp chopped fennel herb
salt to taste

Cooking instructions

1. Mix the black pepper and nuts together.
2. Using a mortar and pestle, pound the garlic into a pulp. Add 1 tsp sea salt and 1 tbsp groundnut oil. Mix into a paste and rub into both sides of the chops.
3. Spread the black pepper and nuts mixture on a clean chopping board; lay the chops, one at a time, on the mixture and bash them on both sides with a kitchen mallet to break up the meat fibres, a process which tenderises the pork.
4. In a skillet or large, thick-bottomed frying pan, heat the remaining groundnut oil until hot. Fry the chops, leaving 1 inch (2½ cm) between them, for 10 minutes each side. Set them aside where they can be kept warm.
5. Lower the heat and pour in the medium dry sherry, stirring to take up the caramelised residue of the chops. Add the grated onion, minced Scotch bonnet pepper and tomato purée, stir to mix well and cook for 2 minutes before adding the stock. Turn up the heat to reduce the liquid a little, add the chopped fennel herb and cream, stir to combine. Taste for seasoning and adjust if needed. Pour the sauce onto the chops and serve immediately. It would go well with sweet potato mash and runner beans.

CURRIED PORK
Serves 4-6

Ingredients

1 kg (2¼ lb) belly pork, some of the fat trimmed, cut into 1½ inch (4 cm)
    cubes, rinsed in lime water (see Miscellany) and drained
1 tsp coarsely ground black pepper
1 tsp mustard seeds
1 tsp cumin seeds
4 tsp Madras curry powder
2 onions, coarsely chopped
3 garlic cloves, finely minced
3 cloves
2 inches (5 cm) cinnamon stick
4 green chillies
1 tbsp lime juice
400 ml (14 fl oz/ ⅔ pt) chicken stock

For marinade

2 tsp sea salt
2 tbsp freshly squeezed lime juice
½ Scotch bonnet pepper, de-seeded and finely minced
1 tbsp clear honey
1 tsp curry powder

Cooking instructions

1. Combine the marinade ingredients in a dish. Add the pork to it, working in the marinade with your hands. Let it marinate for at least 3 hours.

2. In a large heavy-bottomed saucepan, fry the onions until they become translucent and going brown. At this stage add the garlic, so that when the garlic is cooked without burning, the onions are in the right condition, having lost all their moisture, to allow the spices to release their flavour more effectively in the hot oil. Add the black pepper, cinnamon stick, cloves, cumin seeds; fry for 60 seconds, then add the mustard seeds and 2 tsp curry powder; fry for about 10 seconds while stirring.

3. Lift the pork out of its marinade and into the saucepan. Stir vigorously to integrate the pork with the rest of the ingredients. Cook for 10-15 minutes, stirring from time to time; then add the remaining curry powder along with the green chillies. Stir well, add the stock, taste and adjust seasoning if needed. Bring to the boil, lower heat and gently simmer for 1½-2 hours, or until tender. Before lifting off the saucepan, add the lime juice; taste and adjust seasoning before serving with rice or roti.

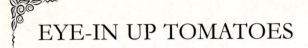

EYE-IN UP TOMATOES

Yuh eye-in up meh tomatoes,
up and dong, yuh lookin so long
yuh makin dem blush;
even the half-ripe ones
turn red, red, red
buh ah tellin yuh
like de folk song said,

mister dohn touch meh tomatoes.

Hans off, Mister dohn squeeze meh tomatoes,
dohn mek dem sorfen.
Buy dem an is yours;
den yuh could do wat yuh want wid dem.
Yuh could squeeze all yuh want to
till dem sorf sorf.
Bite dem if yuh want to
leh de juice run,
suck dem like *Soucouyant*;
or be good, slice dem up,
put dem in a salfish stew.

TOMATO TROTTERS

Spicy and boneless for those who don't like sucking bones and licking fingers.
Serves 4.

Ingredients

6 pig trotters, singed, scrubbed and washed clean in strong
   lemon water (see Miscellany)
1 onion, coarsely chopped
2 cloves garlic, finely minced
1 tsp freshly ground black pepper
1 tbsp black peppercorns
1 tbsp tomato purée
4 tomatoes, peeled and quartered
1 tbsp chopped spring onion green
1 bouquet garni of sage, thyme and chives
1 whole and intact Scotch bonnet pepper
2 tbsp cider vinegar or white wine vinegar
150 ml (5 fl oz/¼ pt) white wine
2 tbsp pig trotter stock
3 tbsp extra virgin olive oil
salt to taste

Cooking instructions

1. Put the pig trotters in a large saucepan with salt, black peppercorns, vinegar, bouquet garni and enough water to cover them by ½ inch (a little over 1 cm). Bring to the boil on moderate heat; lower heat further and simmer gently for 2 hours or until tender. Remove from the saucepan and put aside to cool. With your fingers, pick the meat off the bones; you may use a knife and fork instead. Put aside to add to the tomato sauce later.

2. Heat the olive oil in a saucepan with a thick base until hot. Add onion and fry until translucent and light brown. Stir in the garlic and cook for another 2 minutes before adding tomato purée, ground black pepper, peeled tomatoes and pig trotter meat. Stir to integrate all these ingredients.

3. Pour in the stock and the white wine, add the Scotch bonnet pepper. Taste for seasoning, make adjustments if needed. Lower the heat and simmer for 15-20 minutes to allow the different flavours to come together. Finally, just before serving, remove intact the Scotch bonnet pepper and sprinkle in the spring onion green. This dish goes well with a herb sticky rice.

SPLIT PEAS RICE AND SALTED PIG TAIL

Serves 4-6

Ingredients

225 g (8 oz) salted pig tail (225 g smoked gammon could be used instead)
115 g (4 oz) split peas
170 g (6 oz) long grain rice
1 whole onion, peeled and studded with 7 cloves
2 garlic cloves
1 small onion, finely chopped
1 whole and intact Scotch bonnet pepper
1 bouquet garni of a thyme sprig, rosemary sprig and 3 sage leaves
1 tsp black peppercorns
1 bay leaf
175 ml (6 fl oz) coconut milk
1 tsp freshly ground black pepper
28 g (1 oz) butter
2 tbsp extra virgin olive oil
1 tbsp plain white flour
salt to taste

Cooking instructions

1. Soak salted pig tail or smoked gammon in cold water overnight.

2. Soak split peas overnight, or 3 hours at least.

3. Rinse the pig tail or gammon, put it in a pan with cold water that covers it by about 2 inches (5 cm). Add 1 garlic clove in its bruised skin, peppercorns, the onion studded with cloves and the bouquet garni. Bring slowly to the boil on a medium heat; skim as is necessary. Lower heat and gently simmer for 1½-2 hours, or until pig tail or gammon is tender. Set it aside to cool in its own stock. When cool, cut into 1 inch (2½ cm) cubes; reserve the stock for later.

4. Wash the split peas, put into a saucepan, add water to cover them by 1 inch (2½ cm). Cook on moderate heat until soft enough to be squeezed flat between thumb and forefinger. Drain and set aside.

5. Put the rice to soak for 20 minutes in cold water while the meat and split peas are being cooked. Rinse the rice until the water runs clear. Set it aside.

6. In a large saucepan with a thick base, heat the olive oil until hot, then add the butter. When it melts, remove the saucepan from the heat and stir in the flour. Return to the heat stirring continuously until the roux turns a golden yellow.

7. Add the chopped onion. Cook until it turns translucent. Add the pig tail or gammon. Stir well together before adding the rice. Cook for 1 minute, stirring to prevent sticking; add a little more oil if necessary. Add the stock from the pig tail, coconut milk, ground black pepper, Scotch bonnet pepper and split peas. Cover tightly and cook for 7-10 minutes on low heat. Remove Scotch bonnet pepper, stir once more and serve immediately.

IN A CARIBBEAN RESTAURANT

Wha yuh wan eat?

Jus cook meh
some rice-an-peas
jus like meh granma
use to mek.

Eh?

Listen,
it mus have coconut milk,
an ah piece ah salt-pork fuh flavour,
fresh thyme, Scotch bonnet pepper,
whole, green and intack.
So do meh a favour,
cook it like meh granma
or, you'll get de sack;
an hey, dohn forget
to put rice wid de peas.

Is ok, is ok man,
I only givin yuh
ah bit a *picong*.

SOUPS

Soup, Always a Hearty Trini Food

BREAKFAST SHED AND PEPPER

1

Fo-day morning. City people
still hugged the fusty warmth of bedrooms,
deaf to the yard-cock's fanfare.

Stevedores refuelled on fried king fish, bakes
and greasy cocoa-tea in the Breakfast Shed,
a place of many kitchens a stone-pelt distance away
from big boats moored to Port-of-Spain quay.

These muscled, ebony men saw their mothers
through the steam of pots.
They knew that overnight king fish had revelled
with thyme, Scotch bonnet pepper and shadow beni.
They knew that overnight the spirits of ancestors
had come to taste, to bless flavours of survival.

2

These days the Breakfast Shed draws
a motley crowd, like fowl to a feeding back-yard:
retired civil servants, septuagenarians to a man
and buddies now, make a shit-talk-and-food *lime*,
give fatigue, *mauvais-langue* old bosses
who barred their way up the ladder.

Executives in the flush of business youth,
short sleeves and Trini-island pride,
tuck tie ends away from cow heel soup, coocoo and callaloo,
their maco-talk sharper than the pepper sauce
they spike their food with.

These days Europeans come; not to plant a flag.
Their lust is not for the search of Montezuma's gold,
but the Midas sun. The not-tanned enter slowly.
They linger over the speech rhythms of oral menus;
cooks are patient with amused grins:
'…an above all, mine deh peppersauce,' they say.

The well-tanned beeline to their favourite kitchens,
order stewed king fish in Solomon-ah-gundy sauce
rice and peas, mauby or sorrel to put out fires
raging in their throats.

COW HEEL SOUP
Serves 4-6

Ingredients

2 cow heels, chopped or sawn into 2-3 inch (5-7½ cm) pieces by your
   friendly butcher. (When buying the cow heels, look for the ones
   which are well scraped and cleaned.)
lime water for washing (see Miscellany)
2 large potatoes, peeled and cut into 16 pieces, each approximately 1
   inch (2½ cm)
450 g (1 lb) yam, peeled and cut into 1 inch (2½ cm) chunks
2 red sweet peppers (capsicum)
1 onion, finely chopped
2 celery stalks, de-strung and cut into ½ inch (1¼ cm) pieces
1½ litres (50 fl oz/2½ pt) water
1 whole and intact Scotch bonnet pepper
1 tbsp finely chopped chives
1 tsp chopped parsley
2 tsp salt
2 tsp freshly squeezed lime juice
1 tsp freshly ground black pepper

Cooking instructions

1. Wash cow heels in lime water. Put them into a large saucepan of cold
   water with 2 tsp salt. Bring to the boil, skimming away scum as it rises
   to the surface. Lower heat and simmer for 1 hour or until the meat is
   tender.

2. Remove cow heels from the
   saucepan. Cut all the meat away
   from the bones. Return the
   pieces to the saucepan.

3. Add all the vegetables along with
   the Scotch bonnet pepper. Cook
   until the vegetables are tender.
   Add the chives, parsley, black
   pepper and lime juice. Simmer
   for another 10-15 minutes.
   Remove the Scotch bonnet
   pepper carefully. Taste and adjust
   seasoning if needed and serve
   hot.

COW HEEL SOUP
(On a first visit to Trinidad)

Lips, reluctant to part,
tastebuds peppered,
"It may be savoury,
but it sticks like glue,"
you say.

Buh cowheel soup
dohn stick Trini lips togedder.
Boy, is picong an buss-out larf
an a whole lot ah ole talk
bout aphrodisiacs.

CALLALOO SOUP

From Portuguese **cararú**, a rich soup or stew from calalu leaves; originally Amerin<
caarurú, a thick leaf. Serves 6-8

Mammie, my great-grandmother, a feisty African of Yoruba ancestry, loved her coocoo and callaloo. She made the best coocoo and callaloo this side of heaven. I looked forward to Sundays when it was her custom to perform her culinary magic, cooking a Scotch-bonnet-pepper-hot delicious coocoo and callaloo. It was what she wanted to eat on Sundays when the rest of the family enjoyed my mother's Sunday chicken stew with rice and peas and side dishes of sweet potatoes, yam, ripe plantain and callaloo with crab. I do have to confess that on Sundays I ate the dinner my mother cooked, but also had a substantial taste of Mammie's Sunday favourite.

Traditionally callaloo was made with the large heart-shaped leaves and fleshy stalk of the dasheen tuber, okras (okroes) or ladyfingers as they are known in England. In these modern times, however, when eclecticism rules ok, an acceptable substitute is the humble spinach on its own or muscled up with Swiss chard. The callaloo cooked to a thick consistency, either by reduction or by cooking with less liquid, is the one eaten with coocoo; on the other hand, the thinner, runny variety is the soup. In the final analysis, it all boils down (if you'll forgive the pun) to one's preference.

REAL CALLALOO DOHN COME IN TIN

Every self-respectin Trini know dat dasheen leaf wid de long fleshy stem is gud fuh real callaloo. De leaf is big and shape like a sentimental heart drawn in de transparency of air, den coloured green like de forest in wet season.

In de fresh mornin wen I go to pick dasheen leaf fuh callaloo, yuh see wey de leaf join de long fleshy stem, well, dey is always a small globule of water like a small-small crystal ball. Ah like to ben back de leaf to see how de little crystal ball run on de green leaf, smoode like velvet, jus like quicksilver.

Wid a sharp knife ah cut de stem wid de leaf from de dasheen bush an den go to pick some ochroes an a green Scotch bonnet pepper. De blue crab already in de bucket mekin little bubbles wid he mout. Ah go get im ready fuh de callaloo after ah fine meh lay-lay stick fuh swivellin up de callaloo wen it cook. Ah lay out meh onion, garlic, black pepper, salt and a sprig ah thyme, an ah ready now to cook-up a real callaloo.

Ingredients

225 g (8 oz) each of Swiss chard and spinach; or 450 g (1 lb) spinach,
  coarsely chopped
225 g (8 oz) okras, coarsely chopped
4 rashers of smoked streaky bacon, coarsely chopped
1 onion, finely chopped
1 fat garlic clove, finely minced
1 whole and intact Scotch bonnet pepper
½ tsp de-seeded and finely minced red chilli
1 tsp finely chopped chives
1 tsp dried thyme
crab meat from 1 dressed crab (optional)
850 ml (30 fl oz/1½ pt) vegetable or chicken stock
300 ml (10 fl oz/½ pt) coconut milk
salt to taste
2 tbsp sunflower oil

Cooking instructions

1. Heat the sunflower oil in a large saucepan. Add onion, garlic, chilli and
    bacon; fry for 2 minutes, then pour in the stock and coconut milk. Add
    okras, spinach, thyme, chives and Scotch bonnet pepper. Bring to the
    boil, lower heat and simmer for 15-20 minutes before adding the crab
    meat, if being used.
2. Remove Scotch bonnet pepper; taste and adjust seasoning. Stir vigorously
    to break up the callaloo leaves and give a smoother texture, then serve.

GREAT-GRANNIE MAMMIE'S SUNDAY FOOD

Coocoo and peppery callaloo
was meh great grannie's Sunday meal,
de food fuh she body and she spirit too;

and though de rest of us eat chicken stew,
we still have appetite fuh Mammie's real
coocoo and peppery callaloo.

Wen she reached fuh de pot we knew
de nex ting she go need was some cornmeal
to mek de food fuh she body an she spirit too.

Sundays she was a change woman; she drew
a-lot-ah strent cookin wid ah ritual zeal
she coocoo and peppery callaloo,

an wid each mouthful she eat she grew
in wisdom to cope wid any ordeal.
Dis food fuh she body an she spirit too

did mek she remember Afrika, and renew
she identity; it did mek everytin real.
Coocoo and peppery callaloo
was de food fuh she body an she spirit too.

PRAWN AND MONK FISH BISQUE
Serves 6-8

Ingredients

675 g (1½ lb) monk fish, washed in lime or lemon water (see Miscellany) and cut into 1 inch (2½ cm) cubes
450 g (1 lb) prawns, from which the intestinal vein along the back is removed
6 spring onions, sliced thinly and diagonally
28 g (1 oz) butter
2 tbsp sunflower or corn oil
2 tbsp plain flour
850 ml (30 fl oz/1½ pt) chicken stock
1 tbsp freshly squeezed lemon juice
1 tsp pepper sauce
½ tsp ground black pepper
1 tsp grated root ginger
2 bay leaves
1 whole and intact Scotch bonnet pepper
150 ml (5 fl oz/1¼ pt) whipping cream

Cooking instructions

1. Place the monk fish and prawns in a bowl. Add 1 tsp fine sea salt, 1 tbsp lemon juice and 1 tsp pepper sauce; set aside to marinate for 20-30 minutes.
2. Heat oil in a saucepan. When the oil is hot add the butter, then the flour, stirring constantly to mix in and cook the flour until it becomes a rich yellow. Remove saucepan from the heat and steadily and gradually stir in 300 ml (10 fl oz/½ pt) chicken stock to obtain a smooth mixture.
3. Return the saucepan to the heat and add the remaining stock, stirring all the while. Bring to the boil, lower heat, add black pepper, grated ginger, whole Scotch bonnet pepper and bay leaves; simmer for 10 minutes. Add the monk fish, cook for 5 minutes, then the prawns for another 2 minutes. Finally stir in the cream and spring onions, cook for a further 1-2 minutes. Remove the Scotch bonnet pepper intact, taste the bisque and adjust seasoning if necessary. Serve with buttered toast or French bread.

CREAM OF SPINACH SOUP
Serves 4

Ingredients

675 g (1½ lb) washed spinach
1 large potato, peeled, washed and diced
1 onion, coarsely chopped
2 garlic cloves, coarsely chopped
1 tbsp finely chopped parsley
1 tsp ground cumin
1 tsp freshly ground black pepper
1 tsp caster sugar
1 tbsp sunflower oil
1.1 litre (40 fl oz/2 pts) vegetable or chicken stock
150 ml (5 fl oz/¼ pt) single cream

Cooking instructions

1. Heat sunflower oil in a large saucepan; add chopped onion and fry until translucent and light brown. Add cumin, fry for 10 seconds before adding the diced potato, garlic and black pepper.

2. Add half the stock; bring to the boil, then add the spinach. As the spinach reduces, add the rest of the stock. Cover and cook for 3 minutes. Stir in the caster sugar and chopped parsley; remove the saucepan from the heat and set aside to cool.

3. Taste and adjust seasoning if necessary. Put through a food processor until smooth with the consistency of single cream. Return the saucepan to a gentle heat. Do not bring to the boil. When soup is heated through, stir in the cream and serve immediately.

CHICKEN RICE SOUP
Serves 4

Ingredients

170 g (6 oz) jasmine rice, washed and soaked in water for 15-20
    minutes
170 g (6 oz) chicken breast, washed in lemon water (see Miscellany),
    patted dry and very thinly sliced
6 spring onions, the pale end, thinly sliced
½ tsp finely minced red chilli pepper
1 garlic clove, finely minced
1 tsp freshly squeezed lime juice
1 tbsp chopped coriander
1 tsp sesame oil
1 tbsp peanut oil
1 tbsp dry sherry
75 ml (3 fl oz/4 tbsp) coconut milk
850 ml (30 fl oz/1 ½ pt) chicken stock
1 tbsp light soy sauce
1 level tbsp cornflour
salt to taste

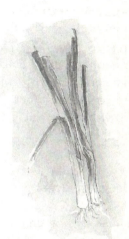

Cooking instructions

1. Put the very thinly sliced chicken in a bowl. Add the dry sherry, sesame oil, red chilli and light soy sauce to the chicken. Stir well into the chicken and leave to marinate for 20-30 minutes.

2. Heat peanut oil in a large saucepan. Add the sliced spring onions and fry for 1 minute before adding the rice and minced garlic. Continue frying for another minute; then add the marinated chicken, stirring to ensure all the ingredients are brought well together.

3. Add the chicken stock; bring to the boil, lower the heat, partially cover the saucepan and simmer for 20-25 minutes.

4. Taste and adjust seasoning if needed. Mix the cornflour with a little water and stir it into the soup. Add the coconut milk and chopped coriander. Cook for another 3 minutes, stir and serve.

ROCKLEY VEGETABLE SOUP
Serves 4-6

Ingredients

2 cloves garlic, finely minced
I large onion, finely chopped
170 g (6 oz) pumpkin, peeled, washed and cut into I inch (2½ cm)
  chunks
½ breadfruit, peeled, washed and cut into I inch (2½ cm) chunks
225 g (8 oz) yam, peeled, washed and cut into chunks
I whole and intact Scotch bonnet pepper
800 ml (28 fl oz) or 2 tins coconut milk
700 ml (25 fl oz/I¼ pt) vegetable stock
I tsp freshly ground black pepper
I large sprig of thyme
2 tbsp coarsely chopped coriander
2 tbsp virgin olive oil
salt to taste

Cooking instructions

1. Heat olive oil on moderate heat and when hot add the onions and fry
   until translucent. Add the garlic and black pepper; fry for about 30 seconds
   before adding the yam, breadfruit and pumpkin. Cook for 2-3 minutes,
   stirring from time to time.
2. Add the stock and coconut milk. Bring to the boil; add the Scotch bonnet
   pepper, sprig of thyme and salt to taste. Cover and cook for 25-30
   minutes or until the vegetables are cooked and not broken up too much.
   Remove the Scotch bonnet pepper, stir in the chopped coriander, adjust
   seasoning if needed and serve.

CREAM OF PIGEON PEAS SOUP

Serves 6-8

Ingredients

450 g (1 lb) pigeon peas, soaked overnight, washed and cooked with a
    bruised clove of garlic until soft (alternatively, 2 tins of ready-cooked
    pigeon peas)
1 litre (35 fl oz/1¾ pt) chicken stock
1 onion, finely chopped
1 garlic clove, finely minced
1 large potato, cut into small dice
1 tbsp plain flour
1 whole and intact Scotch bonnet pepper
1 tbsp chopped parsley
1 tbsp chopped coriander
300 ml (10 fl oz) coconut milk; or 3 tbsp grated cream coconut block
    stirred into ½ pt hot chicken stock
58 g (2 oz) butter
1 tbsp virgin olive oil
1 tsp freshly ground black pepper
salt to taste
150 ml (5 fl oz/¼ pt) single cream

For soup dumplings

115 g (4 oz) cornmeal or polenta
55 g (2 oz) plain flour
¾ tsp fine sea salt
¼ tsp baking powder
salt to taste
1 tbsp sunflower oil
water for mixing

Making dumplings

Put cornmeal, flour, baking powder and salt in a mixing bowl. Make a well
and pour into it the oil and enough water to make non-sticky dough. Knead
the dough until quite smooth. Pinch off small bits of dough and shape, with
the palm of your hands, little dumplings resembling miniature, elongated
rugby balls ready to be added to the soup.

Cooking instructions

1. Heat oil in a large saucepan; add butter and when the butter is melted, add the onion and fry until translucent.

2. Add the garlic and black pepper, fry for 1 minute before adding the flour; stir to mix well with the other ingredients.

3. Stir in the pigeon peas and diced potatoes. Add the stock and coconut milk. Bring to the boil. Drop in the whole Scotch bonnet pepper. Add cornmeal dumplings. Lower heat and cook, stirring from time to time, until potatoes are soft, and the dumplings float. Add the chopped parsley and coriander. Continue cooking for another 5 minutes. Remove carefully the Scotch bonnet pepper, taste and adjust seasoning if needed. Stir in the single cream and serve immediately.

Grinding Yella George

SPLIT PEAS SOUP WITH CORNMEAL DUMPLINGS

Serves 6-8

Ingredients

450 g (1 lb) yellow split peas, washed, soaked overnight and cooked
    with a sprig thyme and 1 clove of garlic until soft
1 large potato, cut into small dice
2 garlic cloves, finely minced
1 onion, finely chopped
1 red sweet pepper, finely chopped
1 tbsp plain flour
2 tbsp virgin olive oil
115 g (4 oz) salted pork, smoked bacon or pancetta
400 ml (14 fl oz/ $^2/_3$ pt) coconut milk
500 ml (16 fl oz) chicken stock
2 sage leaves, coarsely chopped
1 sprig thyme
1 bay leaf
1 whole and intact Scotch bonnet pepper
1 tsp black pepper
salt to taste
cornmeal dumplings (see p.42)

Cooking instructions

1. Heat oil in a large saucepan. Add onion and fry until transparent and
    light brown. Add garlic, sage and salted pork, smoked bacon or pancetta
    and the black pepper. Cook for 2 minutes on moderate heat.

2. Add 1 tbsp plain flour; mix well with the other ingredients. Stir in the
    chopped red sweet pepper and potato. Stir well to bring the ingredients
    together. Pour in the stock and coconut milk; add the cooked split peas;
    thyme, bay leaf and Scotch bonnet pepper. Lower heat, cover and simmer
    30 minutes. Add the cornmeal dumplings. Cook for another 15 minutes.
    Remove carefully the Scotch bonnet pepper, stir and taste for seasoning;
    adjust if needed and serve immediately.

SANCOCHE

From the Spanish, **sancochar**, to parboil. Serves 6-8

Ingredients

675 g (1½ lb) chicken thighs, washed and seasoned with salt, ground
    black pepper, 1 tbsp white rum and set aside for at least 30 minutes
55 g (2 oz) chorizo coarsely chopped
115 g (4 oz) smoked bacon joint, cut into 1 inch (2½ cm) pieces
1 large onion, coarsely chopped
2 garlic cloves, finely minced
2 medium-sized carrots, peeled and coarsely chopped
450 g (1 lb) potatoes, peeled and cut into 1½ inch (4 cm) chunks
450 g (1 lb) yam, peeled and cut into 1½ inch (4 cm) chunks
1 tin of cooked mixed beans or red kidney beans, drained
1 tsp dried thyme
1 tbsp coarsely chopped fresh tarragon or 1 tsp dried tarragon
1 tsp freshly ground black pepper
1 whole and intact Scotch bonnet pepper
1¾ litres (60 fl oz/3 pt) chicken or vegetable stock
2 tbsp sunflower oil
salt to taste

For dumplings

55 g (2 oz) plain flour
115 g (4 oz) cornmeal
½ tsp fine salt
1 tbsp sunflower oil
water for mixing

Cooking instructions

1. Heat oil in a large saucepan on moderate heat. Add the coarsely chopped
    onion. When onion pieces turn translucent, add the garlic, chorizo, smoked
    bacon and black pepper. Fry for 2 minutes, stirring from time to time.
2. Add the seasoned chicken; stir well, cover and cook for about 3 minutes
    before adding the stock, yam and carrots. Turn up the heat to bring
    stock to the boil. Lower heat, add the Scotch bonnet pepper and simmer
    for 30 minutes.
3. While the soup is simmering, mix the dumpling ingredients in a bowl
    to form a ball of dough; knead well. Pinch off very small bits of dough,
    and using the palms of your hands, make little dumplings, resembling
    elongated rugby balls. Drop them gently into the soup.
4. Add the potatoes. When the potatoes are cooked, add the tin of mixed
    beans, thyme and tarragon. Cook for another 5 minutes to allow the
    herbs to infuse into the soup. Remove the Scotch bonnet pepper. Stir,
    taste and adjust seasoning if needed. Serve immediately.

TRINI CHINEEMAMA SOUP
Serves 4-6

It is important to prepare all the ingredients and to put them within easy reach before commencing the actual stir-fry cooking process.

Ingredients

5 Chinese dried mushrooms, washed briefly and soaked in 150 ml (5 fl oz/ ¼ pt) warm water and cut into thin slices
3-5 shitake mushrooms (the larger quantity if small to medium size), cut into thin slices
5-7 oyster mushrooms, the larger ones torn into 3 strips
1 tbsp dried wakame seaweed soaked in 150 ml (5 fl oz/¼ pt) warm water
1-3 pieces of wood ears (edible fungus), depending on size, soaked in warm water for 10-15 minutes, then cut into strips
3 spring onions, thinly sliced
1 tsp grated root ginger
1 garlic clove, finely minced
1 tsp de-seeded, finely minced chilli
1 medium-sized courgette, cut into slivers using a potato peeler
1 medium-sized carrot, cut into slivers using a potato peeler
15 g (½ oz) fine rice noodles
50 g (2 oz) fine egg noodles
½ tsp 5-spice powder
1 litre (35 fl oz/1¾ pt) chicken stock
1 tbsp dry sherry
1 tbsp light soy sauce
¼ tsp caster sugar
2 tsp groundnut oil

Cooking instructions

1. Heat the oil in a large saucepan; add spring onions, grated ginger, garlic and chilli. Stir-fry for 1-2 minutes, then add wood ears (without their soaking water, which is discarded) and Chinese mushrooms (retain their soaking water for later use). Continue to stir-fry for a few seconds. Add the shitake and oyster mushrooms.

2. Add soy sauce, dry sherry, caster sugar and 5-spice powder. Stir well to integrate ingredients. Add chicken stock, seaweed with its water, and the water from the Chinese mushrooms. Bring to the boil; add noodles and slivers of courgette and carrot.

3. Lower heat and simmer for 5-7 minutes or until noodles are cooked. Noodles must not be overcooked. Taste and adjust seasoning if needed. Serve hot.

TOBAGO FISH TEA & TRINI FISH BROTH

Serves 4-6

Fish Tea is not what you may think. It is more broth than tea, *Good fuh de brain,* according to *ole people dem-say.* These two recipes are siblings without the rivalry. They are nonetheless subtly different in taste, and Trini Fish Broth is bulkier. Both are delicious. King fish, red fish or snapper are suitable for both recipes; however, I remember as a boy going to meet the fish trucks in the middle of the night and helping to make Tobago Fish Tea with the anchovies or jacks I had bought.

The ingredients, methods of preparation and cooking are the same, except that with Trini Fish Broth there is the addition of potatoes and macaroni, and instead of chopped chives there is dill and bay leaf.

Ingredients for Tobago Fish Tea

675 g (1½ lb) fish
4 green bananas, peeled, washed in
  lime water and cut into pieces
1 large onion, sliced
1 garlic clove, crushed
1 sprig thyme
1 Scotch bonnet pepper, green
  and intact
1 tsp freshly ground black pepper
4 tbsp lime juice
1 tbsp sunflower oil
1 tsp chopped chives
1.1 litre (40 fl oz/2 pt) water
sea salt to taste
1 tbsp coarsely chopped coriander

Ingredients for Trini Fish Broth

1 kg (2¼ lb) fish
4 green bananas, peeled, washed
  in lime water and cut into pieces
1 large onion, sliced
1 garlic clove, crushed
1 sprig thyme
1 Scotch bonnet pepper, green
  and intact
1 tsp freshly ground black pepper
4 tbsp lime juice
1 tbsp sunflower oil
1 tsp finely chopped fresh dill
1 bay leaf
2 litres (72 fl oz/3½ pt) water
2 large potatoes, each cut into 8
  pieces
170 g (6 oz) macaroni
2 medium-sized tomatoes, peeled
  and cut into quarters
sea salt to taste
1 tbsp coarsely chopped coriander

Cooking instructions

1. Gut, scale and cut the fish into pieces. Wash in 2 tbsp lime juice and water. *(Your friendly fishmonger could be persuaded to gut and scale the fish for you; but just think about it, do you really want to miss out on the fun of doing it yourself?)*

2. Season the fish with 1 tbsp lime juice, sea salt, black pepper and chopped chives (finely chopped dill for Trini Fish Broth). Put aside to marinate for at least 30 minutes.

3. Put a large saucepan on medium heat, add sunflower oil. Fry onions until translucent without going brown, then add garlic and fry for another minute. Add water and vegetables, including tomatoes (if using), then bring to the boil and cook until tender (for Trini Fish Broth, when vegetables are nearly cooked, add macaroni).

4. Add fish, Scotch bonnet pepper, thyme (also bay leaf for Trini Fish Broth) and a little of the marinade. Cook for 15-20 minutes on a gentle heat, after which time, remove very carefully the Scotch bonnet pepper to avoid rupturing it. Taste and adjust seasoning, add the remaining tbsp of lime juice, sprinkle on 1 tbsp coarsely chopped coriander and serve while hot.

HAULING IN THE SEINE

With each rhythmic grunt
the fishermen haul you in.
Spilled out on moon-soaked sand
you are sea harvest now, bewilderment
fixed in your lidless eyes,
gills sucking emptiness.

Fishermen celebrate. They blow
staccato harmonies on conches
calling the fish-tea cooks.

Like night gulls they come in a clamour,
brandishing tin-pans and calabashes.
Before the sun comes up
they will be feasting on fish-tea:

A fish broth
wid some green fig, onion, ah squeeze ah lime,
some thyme an a Scotch bonnet pepper
drop in whole fuh flavour.
Is good fuh de brain
dem ole people say.

Revised version
from *Voices from a Silk-Cotton Tree* (Smith/Doorstop Books)

JL'S FISH CHOWDER
Serves 4-6

Ingredients

1⅓ kg (3 lb) white fish, marinated for 20 minutes in the juice of 1 lime, 1
  tbsp finely chopped dill or chives, salt, 2 tsp turmeric powder and 1
  tsp ground black pepper
225 g (8 oz) smoked haddock, skinned, washed in lime water and rinsed
2 rashers of smoked streaky bacon, cut into pieces
3 potatoes, peeled, washed and each cut in ½ and sliced
5 spring onions (put the very green sections aside for garnishing)
1 tsp finely minced chilli
1 finely chopped garlic clove
1 whole and intact Scotch bonnet pepper
1 sprig of thyme
1 tsp fennel seeds
575 ml (20 fl oz/1 pt) light fish or vegetable stock
300 ml (10 fl oz/½ pt) fresh milk
1 tbsp sunflower oil
salt to taste

Cooking instructions

1. Heat oil in a large saucepan. Fry spring onions for 1 minute. Add fennel
    seeds, garlic, chilli and bacon. Stir and cook for 2 minutes; add potatoes
    and fry for another minute while stirring.

2. Stir in the stock and milk, add the Scotch bonnet pepper. Cook until
    potatoes are soft. Add the marinated fish, the smoked haddock and
    sprig of thyme. Lower heat and simmer for 7-10 minutes. Remove the
    Scotch bonnet pepper, stir well, taste and adjust seasoning if needed.
    Garnish with the green of the spring onions and serve immediately.

VEGETABLE DISHES AND RICE

In Honour of Vegetarians

LA CUISINE DE LAUTREC

1

Henri knows from their hunting
recipes together that Maurice
would kill for a plate of pistou.

It is easy enough boiling
vegetables into anonymity.
Now there is a fretting in the
marmite like a mud volcano.
Henri knows that the pistou paste
is what redeems this potage.

With mortar and pestle
he persuades into polygamy
garlic and basil, tomatoes
steamed, peeled and de-seeded;

but there is trauma
in this ménage à trois,
till gruyère and olive oil
are introduced, and PISTOU!
The paste is made. Henri
stirs it in with a wooden spoon.
(Tasting for adjustments
is superfluous, a mere habit.)

Smiling, he moves to open
the front door. Halfway there,
the doorbell rings. Maurice
waits to be let in.

2

After bottles of port spiced with nutmeg,
a brisk swim in the Seine to clear his head;
then to Le Chat Noir to delight in musk interiors,
crayons merciless as his wit.

Mimi came up, smothered him with softness,
distorted his pince-nez, made him think of mother.
Another bottle of port and maybe
he could entice her to his atelier
with promises of last night's pistou.

Banana Bounty

GREEN FIG CURRY
Serves 4

Ingredients

900 g (2 lb) green figs (green unripe bananas)
I large onion, coarsely chopped
3 garlic cloves, finely chopped
450 g (I lb) undyed smoked haddock, or saltfish (salted dried cod),
    soaked overnight, washed and flaked
½ tsp finely minced Scotch bonnet pepper
2 level tbsp curry powder
I tsp cumin seeds
I tbsp freshly squeezed lime juice
I tsp tomato purée
400 ml (14 fl oz/ ²/₃ pt) coconut milk
3 tbsp sunflower oil

Cooking instructions

1. To prepare the green figs, slit their skin lengthwise along their outer
    curve. Peel away their skins. Wash the peeled figs in lime or lemon
    water to prevent discolouring through oxidisation.

2. In a saucepan or deep frying pan, heat the sunflower oil on moderate
    heat. When hot, fry the onions until translucent; add the cumin seeds
    and fry for 25-30 seconds, or until they begin to release their fragrance.
    Add the curry powder and garlic; stir vigorously to mix the ingredients
    well.

3. Cut the green figs into slices about ¼ inch (½ cm) thick and add to the
    saucepan, along with the tomato purée and Scotch bonnet pepper. Cook
    for 2 minutes, stirring once or twice. Add the coconut milk, bring to
    the boil, lower the heat, cover and simmer until the green figs are cooked.

4. Add the smoked haddock. Cook gently for 7-10 minutes, by which time
    the fish should be cooked just right. Taste for seasoning and adjust if
    needed. Serve immediately with plain boiled rice.

PUFF-UP BREADFRUIT
Serves 4

Ingredients

1 whole breadfruit
2 free-range egg yolks
3 free-range egg whites
1 tsp freshly ground black pepper
115 g (4 oz) grated mature cheddar
58 g (2 oz) butter
150 ml (5 fl oz/¼ pt) milk
salt to taste

Cooking instructions

1. Divide the breadfruit in half with a sharp knife, from stem to base, then divide each half into 2 pieces in the same manner. Cut away the central core and peel the skin. Put the pieces in a saucepan of slightly salted cold water. Set it to boil on moderate heat until cooked.

2. While still hot, mash with a potato masher, adding the milk, butter, black pepper and salt to taste. When the breadfruit is smoothly mashed, beat the egg yolks into it and gradually add the grated cheese. The aim is to achieve a mixture softer than a mash, but not as fluid as a purée. Set aside to cool.

3. Whip up the egg whites until light and fluffy with soft peaks. The whipped egg whites must be almost the same size as the breadfruit mixture. Using a flat wooden spatula, gently fold the egg white into the breadfruit. Transfer to a buttered, straight-sided baking dish; bang the dish once onto your work surface to dispel uneven pockets of air. Place the dish on a pre-heated oven sheet and bake for 25-30 minutes at 205°C/400°F/ gas mark 6. Serve immediately.

BALLED BREADFRUIT
Serves 4

Ingredients

1 whole breadfruit
58 g (2 oz) butter
50 ml (2 fl oz/3 tbsp) hot milk
1 tsp freshly ground black pepper
1 pinch ground nutmeg
2 tbsp coarsely chopped coriander
salt to taste

Cooking instructions

1. Divide the breadfruit in half with a sharp knife, from stem to base, then divide each half into two in the same manner. Cut away the central core and peel the skin. Wash and put into a saucepan of lightly salted cold water. Set to boil on moderate heat until cooked.

2. While still hot, mash with a potato masher, adding the butter, black pepper, nutmeg and hot milk. When mashed, add salt to taste and the chopped coriander. Stir vigorously with a wooden spoon to combine the ingredients.

3. Put into an oiled or greased bowl each portion of breadfruit you intend to serve and, shaking it with a rocking and circular motion, shape it into a ball. Serve with fish in a tomato sauce.

JEANNIE'S SUNNY POTATOES
Serves 4

Ingredients

900 g (2 lb) potato, peeled, washed and cut into 1 inch (2½ cm) cubes
4 tbsp corn oil or sunflower oil
1 tsp cumin seeds
½ tsp mustard seeds
1 generous tsp turmeric powder
½ tsp finely chopped red chilli
3 garlic cloves, finely minced
150 ml (5 fl oz/¼ pt) vegetable or chicken stock
1 spring onion, finely sliced
salt to taste

Cooking instructions

1. Heat oil in a wide, deep frying pan with a lid and thick base. When oil is very hot, add cumin and mustard seeds. When the seeds begin to release their fragrance and pop, toss in the cubed potatoes and fry, stirring to ensure that the hot oil covers all the sides. When the cubes of potato begin to turn brown, add the turmeric powder, garlic and chilli. Stir well to integrate all the ingredients.

2. Add the stock and cover immediately to trap the steam generated. When it dies down, uncover, stir and taste for seasoning; adjust if needed. Cover and lower heat. Cook until the liquid has dried up. Test potatoes to see if they are cooked through. If not quite cooked, add a little boiling water, cover and continue cooking. When cooked, sprinkle in the sliced-up spring onions. Stir and serve immediately.

BUTTER SPINACH
Serves 4

Ingredients

675 g (1 ½ lb) spinach, washed, drained and blanched
1 tbsp olive oil
58 g (2 oz) butter
1 medium onion, very thinly sliced
1 garlic clove, finely minced
115 g (4 oz) almond flakes, toasted a light brown
1 tsp dried chilli flakes
2 tbsp dry sherry
salt to taste
1 tbsp single cream (optional)

Cooking instructions

1. In a heavy-bottomed frying pan, melt on moderate heat the butter with the olive oil. Fry the onion slices until translucent. Add the garlic, frying it for 1 minute before adding the blanched spinach. Stir to mix the ingredients together.
2. Add the dry sherry, chilli flakes and salt to taste. Cook for another 2-3 minutes. Stir in the toasted flaked almonds and single cream, if being used. Serve immediately with boiled rice or use as a side dish to a main course.

SWEET-POTATO-PEANUT-BUTTER MASH

Serves 4-6

Sweet potatoes may be baked in their skins, boiled and mashed, peeled and roasted with other vegetables. However, sweet potatoes cook much faster than other vegetables; timing is therefore crucial.

Ingredients

450 g (1 lb) sweet potato, peeled, washed, cut into chunks of equal size
3 tbsp smooth peanut butter
1 tbsp finely chopped red chilli
¼ tsp ground cinnamon
15 g (½ oz) butter
salt to taste

Cooking instructions

1. Cook sweet potatoes in boiling water for about 10 minutes.
2. Mash sweet potatoes in a mixing bowl along with all the other ingredients. Taste and adjust seasoning if needed. Serve hot. It is particularly delicious with pork.

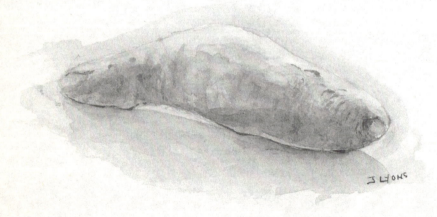

SWEET POTATO PANCAKES
Serves 4

Ingredients

170 g (6 oz) sweet potato, peeled, washed, boiled and mashed
115 g (4 oz) plain flour
575 ml (20 fl oz/1 pt) milk
1 tbsp caster sugar
2 free-range eggs
1 tsp sesame oil
½ tsp ground cinnamon
1 pinch salt
sunflower oil

Cooking instructions

1. In a food processor, mix all the ingredients with the exception of the flour, using half the volume of milk.

2. Pour the puréed sweet potato into a mixing bowl. Sift the flour into it, stirring continuously and adding gradually the rest of the milk to produce a smooth batter which can be easily poured. Set aside for 20-30 minutes.

3. Heat a nonstick frying pan on moderate heat. When frying pan is quite hot, grease with a little oil, covering its entire bottom. Holding the frying pan off the heat, pour in just enough pancake batter for a thin pancake. Incline the frying pan, allowing the flow of batter to cover in a thin layer the entire bottom. Return the frying pan to the heat. Fry pancake, turning once. Potato pancakes are delicious with a filling of honey.

CASSAVA BREAD
Serves 4-6

Cassava is a tropical root vegetable. It is also called *manioc,* an Amerindian word derived from the name of the Arawak male god, Yocohu, reputed to be the giver of *manioc.* There are two types of cassava, bitter and sweet. Only the sweet cassava is sold as a vegetable to be peeled and cooked by boiling. Bitter cassava, on the other hand, is not cooked as a vegetable because of the glucoside poison in it. I hasten to add, however, this poison is dissipated completely when thoroughly cooked by roasting. Bitter cassava is used for the preparation of Cassava farine used in the making of cassava bread, which is dry, flat and unleavened. I remember eating it for breakfast as a child growing up with my grandmother in Tobago. Often as children we also poured hot sweetened milk on Cassava Farine and took great pleasure in seeing it increase in size as it absorbed the sweetened milk.

Using a sharp knife, the bitter cassava is relieved of its brown, leathery skin, washed and grated. The pulp produced by this process is then put into a muslin-like cloth and the starchy juice squeezed out of it. A little more water is mixed with it and squeezed through the cloth again to extract any remaining starch. The mealy residue is then skilfully and gently parched, stirring all the while, traditionally in a cast iron pot on an open fire. When cool it is then stored as Cassava Farine. The container of milky-looking liquid is put aside to allow the starch suspended in it to settle and solidify and put to good use for stiffening white collars and making into a paste. Cassava bread was originally an Amerindian food.

Ingredients

225 g (8 oz/½ lb) Cassava Farine
¼ tsp salt
300 ml (10 fl oz/½ pt) warm water

Cooking instructions

1. Mix all the ingredients in a mixing bowl.
2. Heat a griddle or thick-based frying pan until quite hot. Put 2 tbsp of the mixture on the griddle and flatten with the back of the spoon into a circle ¼ inch (½ cm) thick. Cook until light brown, turn and roast the other side. Set aside covered with a cloth for a flexible bread, or put into the oven at 150°C/300°F/gas mark 2 for a crisp result.

CASSAVA AND BACON PIE

Serves 6-8

Ingredients

900 g (2 lb) sweet cassava, peeled, washed and grated
125 g (4½ oz) streaky bacon, coarsely chopped
2 spring onions, finely chopped
½ red chilli, finely chopped
575 ml (20 fl oz/1 pt) coconut milk
1 tsp freshly ground black pepper
1 tsp dried thyme
1 tbsp sunflower oil
salt to taste

Cooking instructions

1. Fry streaky bacon in sunflower oil until it begins to turn brown; sprinkle in the dried thyme. Remove from the heat.

2. Combine in a large mixing bowl the grated cassava, bacon with the oil in which it was fried, chilli, spring onions, black pepper and coconut milk. Season with a little salt to taste, bearing in mind the bacon's salt content.

3. Transfer the mixture into a well-greased baking dish. Bake in the oven at 190°C/375°F/gas mark 5 until golden brown. Quite delicious accompanied by a tomato salad dressed with virgin olive oil, balsamic vinegar and garnished with coarsely chopped fresh basil.

RIPE PLANTAIN GAMBAGE

Gambage, from the French **gambade** (skip, frolic) is a Creole word meaning 'showing off' or 'creating a diversion'. Serves 4-6.

Ingredients

2 fully ripe plantains, peeled and cut lengthwise into 6 slices (when fully ripe the skin is almost black)
5 green plantains
2 hard-boiled free-range eggs, shelled and coarsely chopped
I spring onion, chopped
½ tsp finely chopped de-seeded Scotch bonnet pepper
½ tsp freshly ground black pepper
I generous pinch grated nutmeg
salt to taste
2 tbsp milk
6 rashers of smoked streaky bacon
sunflower oil for frying

Cooking instructions

1. Using a small paring knife, cut ½ inch (¼ cm) off the tail and stem ends of the green plantains and make a slit in the skin along the outer curve. Put the plantains, in their skins, in a saucepan of cold water over a moderate heat; bring to the boil and cook for 15-20 minutes. When plantains are cooked, they become a dark, brownish green and their skins are split. Drain and set aside to cool so that they can be peeled without discomfort. Chop into small chunks.

2. In a food processor, combine the cooked plantains with hard boiled eggs, spring onions, Scotch bonnet pepper, black pepper, nutmeg, milk and salt to taste. Divide the processed green plantains into 4. Roll each into a sausage shape, 1¼ inches (3 cm) in diameter; divide again into sausage shapes, each 1½ inches (4 cm) long. Put into the refrigerator to firm up.

3. In a large frying pan with a thick base, fry the rashers of bacon in a little hot oil, 2 minutes each side, then put aside.

4. Fry the ripe plantain slices in the same bacon frying pan until they begin to turn brown.

5. Take the green plantain rolls from the refrigerator; roll the streaky bacon around them, followed by the fried ripe plantain slices. Use a toothpick to hold each rolled-up parcel together. Gently fry the parcels on moderate heat to allow the central green plantain to heat through. Serve them immediately on their own, or with a tomato sauce.

YELLA GEORGE AGAIN
(Granma's coocoo)

Yella George
wid corned fish
stewed wid coconut.

Yella George wid
dasheen-leaf callaloo
an a piece ah salt-beef
fuh flavour.

Yella George
sure to fullup hungry hole;
buh take what I tellin yuh,
dohn love Yella George too much,
or he go lie dong heavy on yuh belly
and yuh go have to wash im dong
wid bush tea.

Believe me,
if dat dohn work,
senna pods sure to flush him out good.

Grine de carn, bwoi,
yuh better grine de carn
fuh mek Yella George
to give yuh more strent
to grine carn.

Revised from *Lure of the Cascadura*
(Bogle-L'Ouverture Publications Ltd)

Yella George was the name we children gave to the cornmeal dish we made with the dried and ground maize. See page 136 for a drawing of the reluctant grinder of corn at work.

YELLA GEORGE
Serves 4-6

Ingredients

450 g (1 lb) medium ground cornmeal
850 ml (30 fl oz/1½ pt) coconut milk
2 tbsp corn oil
1 tsp freshly ground black pepper
1 onion, finely chopped
1 tbsp finely chopped chives
salt to taste

Cooking instructions

1. Heat the corn oil in a heavy saucepan. When oil is hot fry onions until translucent. Add black pepper, chives, coconut milk and salt to taste. Bring to the boil.

2. Add the cornmeal all at once while stirring with a wooden spoon. Reduce heat, cover and cook gently for 10 minutes, stirring from time to time. When Yella George is cooked the wooden spoon, stuck in the middle, should keep a vertical position for about 5 seconds. Serve immediately. Delicious with Saltfish with Okra and Tomatoes (see p.61).

BOYOBOY DUMPLINGS

Serves 8-10

Could be used in soup or served with fish in spicy tomato sauce.

Ingredients

2 grated corn on the cob
2 rashers of streaky bacon, fried and chopped (optional)
1 spring onion, finely chopped
1 tsp finely chopped chilli
1 tsp caster sugar
1 tsp fine sea salt
1 tbsp olive oil
150 ml (5 fl oz/¼ pt) water, or preferably coconut milk
170 g (6 oz) self-raising flour
½ tsp baking powder

Cooking instructions

1. Grate the corn on the cob into a large mixing bowl. Add the chilli, spring onion, sugar, salt, olive oil and fried chopped bacon, if being used. Mix well together while adding the coconut milk or water.

2. Add to the self-raising flour the baking powder and sift it into the corn mixture. Use a wooden spoon to bring the ingredients together. Knead to a non-sticky dough, adding more liquid or flour as you deem necessary. Put aside to rest for 10-15 minutes.

3. Roll out the dough into a long sausage shape about 1 inch (2½ cm) in diameter. Divide again into 1½ inch (4 cm) lengths of dough. Transform into any shape you desire and cook in boiling water. Dumplings always increase in size and float up to the surface when cooked, so use a large saucepan to allow for this.

YAMS

Historically, yam was a staple food in the diet of Caribbean slaves. It comes under the inclusive term, 'ground provisions', which also represents several varieties of root vegetables or tubers, including: cassava (or *manioc*), dasheen, tanias, eddoes, sweet potatoes.

Slaves, who were attached to plantation houses, were given a portion of ground to cultivate for their provision of food, hence the term 'ground provision'. This term is still used today in Trinidad and Tobago markets, especially by the older folk. It includes everything grown in the vegetable garden from yams to tomatoes and runner beans.

I remember growing up as a boy in Tobago being sent by my grandmother to dig up yams, which on our land grew wild as a happy, wayward vine, attaching itself to anything growing in its path. Digging up those wild yams, of the yellow-flesh variety, was a very delicate operation. They were often about twelve inches long. My grandmother's instruction was to dig them up whole and intact without any bruises. This entailed using my hands after the initial loosening of the soil around the yam with a garden fork. I had to carefully scrape away the soil from around the exposed yam, particularly at its lower depth where it narrowed and could easily break.

Looking back much later on my yam-digging activities, with poetic licence, I think of the experience as the earth giving birth to yams with my nervous assistance.

Yams, as all other varieties of tubers, can be cooked and prepared in different ways. They can be boiled, roasted, mashed as one does ordinary potatoes and/or made into soufflés; they can also be used in soups. Yam's versatility lends itself to creative culinary experimentation.

CHEEKY YAM SOUFFLÉ
Serves 4

Ingredients

115 g (4 oz) yam
40 g (3 tbsp) butter
200 ml (7 fl oz) coconut milk
3 anchovy fillets, very finely minced
1 tsp capers, finely chopped
¼ tsp finely minced Scotch bonnet pepper
1 tsp finely chopped chives
1 pinch nutmeg
4 free-range egg yolks, lightly beaten
4 free-range egg whites, whipped to soft peaks
60 g (4 tbsp/2 oz) plain flour
butter for greasing soufflé bowl
salt to taste

Cooking instructions

1. Cook yam in boiling water. Using a food processor, pureé yam with butter, coconut milk, capers, anchovies, chilli pepper, chives, egg yolks and a pinch of nutmeg.

2. Pour into a mixing bowl. Sift flour into the mixture to produce a panada the consistency of whipped cream (adjust with coconut milk if needed). It is important to taste the panada for seasoning, since it is this element of the dish which provides the full flavour of the soufflé.

3. Use butter to thoroughly grease the soufflé dish, particularly the straight sides. Dust with flour.

4. Beat a little of the egg white into the panada, then gently and quickly fold in the beaten egg whites, a little at a time, to produce a light air-filled mixture. Transfer the mixture to the greased dish. Bang the dish once, sharply, onto the table to dispel uneven pockets of air.

5. Place the dish on a pre-heated oven tray and bake for 25-30 minutes at 205°C/400°F/gas mark 6. Serve the soufflé immediately while it is still cheekily risen.

HOW TO MAKE A YAM-MASH

Wash off de birt-dirt
from a cush-cush yam;
peel wid a sharp knife
skin stained wid ert.

Cut-up de yam,
wash it again; cook it
in a pan-a-boilin water.

Den, wile it still hot,
mash it up
wid a bit-a-butter,
add salt an pepper.

Use ah wooden spoon
to stir in some hot milk,
buh not much, an soon
yam good to nyam and lick.

MASH YAM FRITTERS
Serves 4-6

Ingredients

150 g (5½ oz) plain flour
300 g (10½ oz) yam
1 free-range egg, lightly beaten
1 tsp freshly ground black pepper
¼ tsp ground nutmeg
1 clove garlic, finely minced
1 spring onion, finely chopped
28 g (1 oz) melted butter
75 ml (3 fl oz/4 tbsp) milk
salt to taste
sunflower oil for frying

Cooking instructions

1. Peel, wash and divide the yam into even-sized chunks. Boil with a little salt until cooked; using a potato masher, crush with butter, black pepper, nutmeg and salt to taste.

2. Add to the mashed yam, garlic, spring onion, egg and milk. Mix thoroughly until smooth. Add flour and continue to mix into dough.

3. In a deep frying pan on moderate heat, fry tablespoons of the dough until golden brown. Serve hot or cold.

I LOVE NYAM YAM
(Definitions)

Nyam-yam: n.
A dish of yam
mashed with butter,
salt and black pepper
(a dusting of nutmeg, optional).

To nyam-yam: vb (tr)
What children do
when they eat-up
a plate of yam-mash
in one minute and a half,
licking the plate until
they see reflections;
then ask for more.

CURRIED NIAM-YAM

Serves 4-6

Ingredients

450 g (1 lb) yam, peeled, washed and cut into 1 inch (2½ cm) cubes
1 onion, coarsely chopped
3 cloves garlic, finely chopped
1 tsp cumin seeds
1 tbsp curry powder
3 tbsp sunflower oil
300 ml (10 fl oz/½ pt) chicken stock
1 tsp freshly squeezed lime juice
1 tsp finely chopped chilli
salt to taste
1 tbsp coarsely chopped coriander

Cooking instructions

1. Half cook yam in boiling water. Drain and set aside.

2. In a deep frying pan with a lid, fry the cumin seeds in hot sunflower oil until they begin to release their fragrance. Add the onions and fry until translucent. Add the garlic and diced yam; continue frying for 10-15 minutes, stirring from time to time to prevent sticking.

3. Mix curry powder with 1 tbsp water and add to the yam. Stir well, pour in the chicken stock, bring to the boil, lower the heat, cover and cook until most of the liquid has evaporated and the yam pieces are soft. Add finely chopped chilli and lime juice. Garnish with the chopped coriander and serve immediately.

STYLISH COOCOO
Serves 4

Ingredients

450 g (1 lb) cornmeal (polenta)
170 g (6 oz) okras, washed, stem end cut off
   and the rest cut into 1½ inch (4 cm) slices
58 g (2 oz) butter
1 small onion, very finely chopped
1 tsp finely minced chilli
1 red sweet pepper (capsicum)
2 tbsp sunflower oil
salt to taste
700 ml (25 fl oz/1¼ pt) boiling hot water

Cooking instructions

1. In a cast iron pot or thick-based saucepan on moderate heat, fry in sunflower oil the onions until translucent, but not brown. Add the okras and cook for 1 minute. Add the chilli, red sweet pepper, butter and salt. Stir and cook for 2 minutes. Add hot water; stir and taste for seasoning; adjust if needed.

2. When the water begins to boil, add the cornmeal all at once in a slow, steady stream and constantly stirring with a wooden spoon to avoid it being lumpy. Lower heat, continue to cook, stirring vigorously. The cornmeal and okras soon become a sticky ball. When the wooden spoon, pushed vertically through the middle of the coocoo ball, remains upright, it is ready to be shaped for serving.

3. Put 1 tbsp of sunflower oil or melted butter into a bowl. Using a large serving spoon, put ¼ of the coocoo into the bowl, shake it with a circular movement to form a ball. Repeat the process until 4 balls are formed. Serve immediately with callaloo.

PICONG POLENTA PIE
Serves 8-10

Ingredients

1 kg (2¼ lb) polenta (cornmeal)
50 g (2 oz) desiccated coconut
1 onion, finely chopped
1 clove garlic, finely minced
250 ml (8 fl oz/ ⅓ pt) hot water
850 ml (30 fl oz/1 ½ pt) coconut milk
115 g (4 oz) butter, melted
½ Scotch bonnet pepper, de-seeded and finely minced
1 tsp black pepper, freshly ground
1 tbsp chives, finely chopped
1 tsp curry powder
1 tbsp sunflower oil
28 g (1 oz) butter
150 ml (5 fl oz/¼ pt) vegetable stock

Cooking instructions

1. In a large mixing bowl mix thoroughly the following ingredients together: the polenta, desiccated coconut, chives and Scotch bonnet pepper. Add the coconut milk and hot water, stir well and put aside for 30 minutes.

2. Sauté in a frying pan on moderate heat the finely chopped onion in 1 tbsp sunflower oil and 1 oz (30 g) butter. When the onion turns translucent, add black pepper and curry powder; stir for 5 seconds before adding the garlic and vegetable stock. Cook for 1 minute. Add to the bowl of polenta along with the melted butter. Stir well to integrate all the ingredients, add salt to taste. The mixture must not be dry. Add more water if needed to produce a consistency resembling a very thick soup.

3. Transfer the mixture to a greased baking dish and bake in a pre-heated oven at 180°C / 350°F/gas mark 4 for 1 hour or until the testing knife is withdrawn cleanly. This pie must be left to cool and served just warm. It is equally delicious eaten cold.

DEEP-FRIED OKRAS
Serves 2-4

Ingredients

250 g (8 oz) okras, washed, their stem end trimmed
sunflower oil or groundnut oil for deep frying
2 tsp sesame oil
3 tbsp lime or lemon juice
2 tbsp light soy sauce
2 tbsp plain flour
1 tsp mustard powder
3 tbsp cornmeal (polenta)
1 free-range egg, beaten

Cooking instructions

1. Mix together the plain flour and mustard powder in a small transparent plastic bag.
2. Put the cornmeal in a shallow bowl; beat the egg in another, set aside conveniently at hand.
3. Toss the okras in a mixture of sesame oil, lime or lemon juice and light soy sauce.
4. Heat 1 inch (2½ cm) depth of oil in a wok until quite hot. Dust a few okras at a time in the plastic bag of flour; dip them into the beaten egg, then roll them in dish of cornmeal.
5. With a pair of kitchen tongs, gently lay the okras in the hot oil. Fry for 30-45 seconds and arrange them on kitchen paper towels without touching each other. Serve with natural yoghurt seasoned with salt, black pepper and finely chopped chives.

VEGETABLE CURRY
Serves 6-8

Ingredients

115 g (4 oz) French runner beans
115 g (4 oz) green garden peas
2 sweet red peppers (capsicum), coarsely chopped
2 sweet green peppers (capsicum), coarsely chopped
115 g (4 oz) carrots, cut into ½ inch (1 cm) dice
285 g (10 oz) potatoes, cut into 1 inch (2½ cm) cubes
1 green chilli, de-seeded and finely minced
1 large onion, chopped
3 garlic cloves, finely chopped
2 tbsp curry powder
1 tbsp cumin seeds
3 tbsp sunflower oil
575 ml (20 fl oz/1 pt) light vegetable stock or water
2 tbsp chopped coriander
salt to taste

Cooking instructions

1. In a large saucepan with a thick base, fry the cumin seeds in hot sunflower oil. When they begin to release their flavour, add the chopped onion and fry until translucent and turning light brown.

2. Add the curry powder, fry for 1 minute while stirring. Add the red peppers, carrots, garlic, potatoes and chilli. Stir vigorously to integrate all the ingredients.

3. Stir in the stock or water. Bring to the boil; then cook on moderate heat for 15-20 minutes, or until the potatoes are cooked. Add the French beans, sweet green peppers and green peas.

4. Continue cooking for another 7-10 minutes. Taste for seasoning and adjust if needed.

5. Add the coriander, remove the curry from the heat and leave to rest for 10-15 minutes before serving with plain boiled rice.

COCONUT RICE AND GREEN PEAS

Serves 4-6

Ingredients

450 g (1 lb) rice
170 g (6 oz) green garden peas
1 garlic clove, finely minced
1 large onion, finely chopped
1 whole and intact Scotch bonnet pepper
2 bay leaves
1 tsp freshly ground black pepper
900 ml (32 fl oz / 1²/₃ pt) coconut milk; or 2 tins (400 ml each) of
   coconut milk plus 100 ml (4 fl oz) water
2 tbsp groundnut oil or sunflower oil
salt to taste

Cooking instructions

1. Wash rice twice, or under the cold tap until water runs clear. Put to
   soak in a bowl of cold water for 15-20 minutes.
2. Heat oil in a heavy-bottomed saucepan, stir in the chopped onion and
   fry until translucent. Add black pepper and garlic and fry for 10 seconds
   before adding the coconut milk. Add salt to taste.
3. Bring to the boil, then add the rice, green peas, bay leaves and Scotch
   bonnet pepper. Cover, reduce the heat to low and cook for 7 minutes,
   or until all the liquid is absorbed and the grains of rice soft.
4. Remove from the heat, take away the Scotch bonnet pepper intact,
   then fluff up with a fork and serve.

OKRA RICE
Serves 4

Ingredients

225 g (8 oz) long grain rice, washed and left to soak in water for 10
    minutes
170 g (6 oz) okras, trimmed and cut into ½ inch (1 cm) slices
2 rashers smoked streaky bacon (optional)
1 onion, finely chopped
1 garlic clove, finely chopped
1 sprig thyme or ½ tsp dried thyme
1 whole and intact Scotch bonnet pepper
250 ml (8 fl oz) vegetable or chicken stock
100 ml (4 fl oz) coconut milk
2 tbsp sunflower oil
salt to taste

Cooking instructions

1. Heat the sunflower oil in a large saucepan, add garlic and chopped onion
    and fry until the onions turn translucent. Add bacon (if being used).
    Fry for another 3 minutes before adding the okras. Stir in the stock
    and coconut milk. Taste and adjust seasoning.
2. Bring to the boil; add the rice, Scotch bonnet pepper and thyme. Stir,
    cover the saucepan, lower heat and cook for 10 minutes or until the
    rice grains are soft. Remove the Scotch bonnet pepper intact before
    serving.

CREOLE FRIED RICE
Serves 6-8

Ingredients/preparation

225 g (8 oz) long grain rice, washed until water runs clean, soaked in cold water for 10 minutes, then boiled in 1 litre (2 pt) of water with a little salt and a few drops of oil for 6-7 minutes. Drain rice through a sieve, pass cold water through it to stop it cooking, fluff up with a fork and set aside.

In a small frying pan on medium heat, dry roast the following: 3 cloves, 9 grains of allspice, ¾ inch (2 cm) piece of cinnamon stick, ¼ tsp fennel seeds, ½ tsp dried chilli flakes. When the spices begin to release their fragrance, transfer to a mortar and with a pestle, crush to make a Creole 5 spice powder.

170 g (6 oz) chicken thighs or fillet steak, washed in lemon or lime water (see Miscellany), cut into very thin slices.

In a mixing bowl beat 1 free-range egg white, 1 tbsp corn flour, 1 tbsp dry sherry and 1 tsp of the Creole 5 spice powder.

Rest of ingredients

2 garlic cloves, finely minced
1 large carrot, peeled and cut into very thin slices
1 large sweet green pepper (capsicum), coarsely chopped
1 large sweet red pepper (capsicum), cut into thin strips
115 g (4 oz) cooked green peas
3 spring onions, sliced
3 free-range eggs, beaten
2 tsp sesame oil
½ Scotch bonnet pepper, de-seeded and finely minced
groundnut oil for frying
light soy sauce for flavouring and seasoning
brown sugar

Cooking instructions

1. Add the sliced, dry-seasoned meat to the egg white marinade and mix thoroughly. Set aside for 10-15 minutes.

2. Heat 1 tbsp groundnut oil on high heat in a large wok until it begins to smoke. Add 1 tsp brown sugar and the moment it begins to caramelise, add some of the meat and stir fry for 1 minute. (It is advisable to cook the meat in batches to prevent the release of juices; this would of course entail the addition of more oil and sugar for each batch.) Set fried meat aside.

3. Scramble-fry the beaten egg in the same wok, adding a little more oil; set aside.

4. Add 1 tbsp groundnut oil to the wok. When hot, stir fry the vegetables starting with the garlic, thinly sliced carrot and the strips of sweet red pepper. After 1 minute, add the meat, spring onions and finely minced Scotch bonnet pepper. Stir-fry for another 2 minutes before adding the sweet green pepper and green peas. Season with soy sauce and flavour with a little sesame oil. Cook for another minute or two.

5. Add the rice and scrambled egg. Stir gently with a folding movement of the stir-fry spoon to bring all the ingredients happily together. Continue cooking for another 5 minutes, stirring once. Taste and adjust seasoning by the addition of soy sauce and serve.

SPINACH RICE
Serves 4

Ingredients

225 g (8 oz) basmati rice, washed and soaked in cold water for 10
    minutes
1 medium-sized onion, finely chopped
1 garlic clove, finely minced
225 g (8 oz) spinach
250 ml (8 fl oz / $^1/_3$ pt) vegetable stock
1 tsp turmeric powder
1 tbsp sunflower oil
knob of butter

Cooking instructions

1. Wash spinach, drain and chop coarsely.
2. Heat oil in a large saucepan. Fry chopped onion until the pieces turn translucent and light brown. Add the rice along with the garlic and turmeric powder, stir and fry for 1 minute before adding the vegetable stock.
3. Bring the stock to the boil, add the spinach, cover tightly, lower the heat to its lowest level and cook for 10 minutes.
4. Uncover saucepan and stir to integrate the rice and the spinach. Taste and adjust seasoning if needed; add a generous knob of butter, cover and leave for 5 minutes before serving.

A TRINI FRIED RICE
Serves 4-6

Ingredients

170 g (6 oz) long grain rice, washed and cooked in plenty of water to
keep grains separate

2 chicken breasts, thinly sliced and marinated for 20 minutes in 1 egg
white, lightly beaten with 1 tbsp dry sherry mixed with 2 tsp corn
flour and 1 tsp black pepper (reserve the egg yolk for the omelettes)

3 omelettes, made with the reserved egg yolk and 2 whole eggs beaten
with a pinch of nutmeg, 1 tsp fine salt, ½ tsp freshly ground black
pepper and 3 drops of sesame oil; cooked and cut into thin strips

115 g (4 oz) green garden peas, cooked for 3 minutes, strained and
passed briefly under cold running water

115 g (4 oz) cooked ham, cut into thin strips

85 g (3 oz) beansprouts, washed and drained

2 spring onions, thinly sliced

1 onion, thinly sliced

1 garlic clove, finely minced

½ red chilli pepper, de-seeded and finely
chopped

2 tsp sesame oil

2 tbsp light soy sauce

2 tsp 5-spice powder

groundnut oil for frying

Cooking instructions

1. Gather the above ingredients within easy reach, then heat 2 tbsp
groundnut oil in a wok or large, deep frying pan until quite hot. Quickly
stir-fry the chicken, in small batches for 1 minute at a time, adding more
oil when necessary.

2. In the same wok or frying pan, stir-fry the sliced onion, garlic and strips
of ham for 1 minute, then add chicken, chilli, 5-spice powder, sesame
oil and soy sauce; stir-fry for another 2 minutes to integrate all the
ingredients.

3. Add the cooked rice, green peas, beansprouts, strips of omelette and
sliced spring onions. Continue to stir-fry vigorously for another 3 minutes,
adding more light soy and sesame oil as you wish. Serve immediately.

RICE WITH KIDNEY BEANS

Serves 4

Ingredients

170 g (6 oz) long grain rice, washed and soaked in cold water for 10-15
  minutes
1 tin kidney beans or 170 g (6 oz) dried kidney beans soaked overnight
  then cooked until soft
1 red sweet pepper (capsicum), finely chopped
1 large carrot, cut into small dice
1 onion, finely chopped
1 garlic clove, finely minced
½ red chilli, de-seeded and finely minced
1 whole and intact green Scotch bonnet pepper
1 tbsp chopped chives
1 tsp paprika
350 ml (12 fl oz) coconut milk
2 tbsp sunflower oil
salt to taste

Cooking instructions

1. Heat sunflower oil in a saucepan. Add onion and fry until translucent
   before adding the garlic and rice. When the grains of rice begin to turn
   white, add the sweet pepper, diced carrots, red chilli and paprika. Stir
   to combine these ingredients.

2. Stir the coconut milk into the rice; bring to the boil, add the Scotch
   bonnet pepper, 1 tsp salt, cooked kidney beans and chopped chives.
   Turn the heat to very low, cover tightly and cook for 10 minutes, or
   until rice grains are soft. Remove intact the Scotch bonnet pepper. Taste
   and adjust seasoning if needed. Stir well, cover the saucepan, turn off
   the heat and leave covered for 2-3 minutes before serving.

YELLOW SPLIT PEAS RICE WITH BACON
Serves 4

Ingredients

225 g (8 oz) smoked gammon, cut into ¾ inch (2 cm) dice
225 g (8 oz) long grain rice, washed and soaked in cold water for 10-15
  minutes
170 g (6 oz) yellow split peas, soaked overnight and cooked until soft
1 onion, finely chopped
1 garlic clove, finely minced
1 whole and intact Scotch bonnet pepper
1 red chilli, de-seeded and finely minced (optional)
1 sprig thyme or 1 tsp dried thyme
2 sage leaves, finely chopped
500 ml (16 fl oz) coconut milk
¼ tsp grated nutmeg
1 generous tsp turmeric powder
2 tbsp sunflower oil
salt to taste

Cooking instructions

1. Heat sunflower oil in a large saucepan. Add onion, garlic and smoked
    gammon. Fry for 10 minutes, stirring from time to time. Add the chopped
    sage and red chilli (if being used). Continue cooking for another minute
    before adding the rice along with the turmeric powder. Stir well.

2. Add the coconut milk and nutmeg; bring to the boil, add the Scotch
    bonnet pepper and thyme. Turn the heat down quite low and cook
    the rice for 3 minutes, then add the cooked split peas. Cover tightly
    the saucepan and continue cooking until the liquid dries up and the
    rice grains are soft. Taste and adjust seasoning if needed. Remove the
    whole Scotch bonnet pepper without rupturing it. Serve immediately.

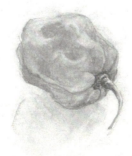

PIGEON PEAS WITH SALTED PORK

Serves 4-6

Ingredients

450 g (1 lb) dried pigeon peas, soaked overnight
250 g (½ lb) salted pork or bacon shank, soaked overnight to remove
   salt
1 large onion, coarsely chopped
2 garlic cloves, finely minced
1 garlic clove, bruised
1 whole and intact Scotch bonnet pepper
1 tbsp chives, finely chopped
1 tsp freshly ground black pepper
3 cloves
2 bruised sage leaves
1 sprig of thyme
575 ml (20 fl oz/1 pt) coconut milk
2 tbsp sunflower oil
salt to taste

Cooking instructions

1. Drain the pigeon peas from their overnight soak and rinse. Put in a saucepan with 1 pint of cold water and a bruised garlic clove, bring to the boil and cook until tender and soft. Set aside.

2. Heat 2 tbsp sunflower oil in a heavy-bottomed pot, and fry onion until translucent and turning brown. Add salted pork (chopped into 1½ inch (4 cm) chunks), garlic, black pepper and cloves to the onions; cook for 10 minutes, stirring from time to time, before adding the coconut milk, thyme, sage and whole and intact Scotch bonnet pepper. Cover and simmer until salted pork is tender.

3. Add the cooked pigeon peas. Stir well to integrate with the pork. Taste and adjust seasoning. Continue cooking for another 10 minutes. Serve with boiled rice or your favourite ground provisions.

PASTA AND SALADS

Your Good Health

SMOKED FISH PASTA
Serves 4

Ingredients

225 g (8 oz) fusilli pasta
225 g (8 oz) undyed smoked haddock
I red onion, thinly sliced
I red chilli, de-seeded and finely chopped
I garlic clove, finely minced
¼ tsp fennel seeds and ½ tsp black peppercorns, dry roasted for 30
  seconds and ground together into a fine powder
28 g (I oz) butter
I tbsp virgin olive oil
I tsp tomato purée
I tbsp coarsely chopped flat leaf parsley
150 ml (5 fl oz/¼ pt) medium sweet white wine
150 ml (5 fl oz/¼ pt) whipping cream
salt to taste

Cooking instructions

1. In a deep frying pan poach the smoked haddock in lemon water for 10
    minutes. Remove the haddock and rinse it in cold water. Carefully flake
    the fish while looking for and discarding any bones found. Set the flaked
    haddock aside.

2. Heat in deep frying pan I tbsp olive oil and butter. Add onion and garlic;
    fry onion until it becomes translucent; stir in the tomato purée, chilli
    and the powdered fennel and black pepper. Add the wine, stir and simmer
    for 2 minutes before adding the flaked fish.

3. Bring a half-filled, large saucepan of lightly salted cold water, with I
    tbsp olive oil, to the boil. Add the pasta; return the water to a rolling
    boil with the saucepan uncovered. When the pasta is cooked soft but
    still firm to the bite, strain through a sieve and add it, along with the
    cream, to the haddock in its sauce. Gently mix the pasta and the sauce
    together, garnish with the chopped parsley and serve immediately.

MACARONI PIE

Serves 4-6

Ingredients

225 g (8 oz) macaroni, cooked in salted water and drained
6 free-range eggs
55 g (2 oz) grated gruyère
85 g (3 oz) grated parmesan
150 ml (5 fl oz/¼ pt) milk
a pinch of freshly grated nutmeg
¼ tsp freshly ground black pepper
½ thinly sliced onion
butter

Cooking instructions

1. In a mixing bowl beat lightly the 6 eggs with milk, grated nutmeg and freshly ground black pepper.

2. Grease generously an oven-proof dish of a size judged suitable for the cooked macaroni.

3. In a large mixing bowl, bring together the cooked macaroni, grated parmesan and the egg and milk. Mix well with a wooden spoon and put the mixture in the buttered oven-proof dish. Top with a layer of the very thinly sliced onion covered with the grated gruyère.

4. Place on a pre-heated, flat oven tray and bake in the oven at 205°C/400°F/gas mark 6 for 25-30 minutes. This pie may be eaten hot or cold; either way it is delicious, especially with a spicy tomato sauce.

My very first taste of macaroni pie was a delicious, belly-filling, pleasurable experience on a clear-blue-sky, shadow-dancing, hot day in Maracas Bay on the north coast of Trinidad. I was a restless, fun-loving teenager with my equally fun-loving, picong-giving school buddies. There were four of us, Ronald, Noel, John and I. We were given the name, The Three Musketeers by our school teachers. We were inseparable to the extent that the teachers often got our names mixed up.

On this glorious day of wind, sparkling sea and huge breakers pounding Maracas Bay's golden sands, we were having a picnic. We all brought a dish to share: chicken pelau, dhalpurie, cassava pone and the macaroni pie brought by John. We ate huge chunks of it and washed it down with sorrel and ginger beer. Needless to say, nothing was left uneaten. Happy, happy, carefree days.

SEAFOOD SALAD
Serves 4

Ingredients

225 g (8 oz) monk fish
170 g (6 oz) cooked tiger prawns
170 g (6 oz) baby squid
225 g (8 oz) mussels
8 oysters
¾ of 1 cucumber, thinly sliced
¼ remaining cucumber, grated
1 red onion thinly, sliced in rings
40 ml (2 tbsp) lime juice
2 red chillies, de-seeded and cut into thin strips
salt to taste
olive oil
shredded lettuce

Cooking instructions

1. Rinse the monk fish, tiger prawns and baby squid in cold water and place in a steamer. Take the beards away from the mussels, scrub and rinse them along with the oysters. Place in the same steamer. Steam for 3-4 minutes. Discard any mussels which have not opened.

2. Cut up the monk fish into small dice. With an oyster knife, remove the oysters and the mussels from their shells. Shell the prawns, discarding the heads and removing the intestinal threadlike vein that runs along the back. Put all the fish together in a salad bowl.

3. Add the grated cucumber with its juice, lime juice, chilli, sliced onion, thinly sliced cucumber and salt to taste. Mix all together and set aside in the refrigerator for at least 30 minutes before serving in individual plates on a bed of shredded lettuce leaves drizzled with olive oil.

CABBAGE AND BACON SALAD

Serves 4

Ingredients

1 green spring cabbage, core removed and green leaves finely shredded
170 g (6 oz) fresh pineapple, cut into small dice
4 rashers of streaky bacon, cut into ½ inch (1 cm) strips and fried till
    crisp but not burnt
½ red chilli, de-seeded and finely chopped
1 tbsp freshly squeezed lemon juice
75 ml (3 fl oz/4 tbsp) whipping cream
½ tsp Dijon mustard
salt to taste

Cooking instructions

1. In a salad bowl mix with your hands the cabbage, pineapple and chilli
    (be careful to wash the chilli oil residue from your fingers after this
    mixing).
2. In a smaller bowl combine whipping cream, lemon juice, Dijon mustard
    and salt. Add to the cabbage and mix well with fork and spoon. Sprinkle
    on the crispy bacon and serve.

MANGO AND VEG SALAD
Serves 4

Ingredients

1 green or nearly-ripe mango, peeled and shaved into slivers with a
    potato peeler
4 tomatoes, each cut into 6 wedges and seeds removed
1 carrot, peeled and cut into thin matchsticks about 2 inches (5 cm) long
1 medium-sized courgette, washed and shaved into slivers with a potato
    peeler or sliced very thinly with a very sharp knife (watch your
    fingers)
juice of 1 lime
2 tbsp sunflower or grape seed oil
½ tsp finely chopped red chilli (optional)
½ tsp caster sugar
salt to taste
1 tsp finely chopped mint

Cooking instructions

1. Combine in a salad bowl the tomatoes, courgettes, carrots and mango.
2. Mix together in a small bowl the oil, lime juice, sugar, salt and chilli (if
    being used) to form an emulsion. Pour over the mango and vegetables.
    Mix well together, garnish with the chopped mint and serve.

MANGO AND APPLE SALAD WITH PARMA HAM
Serves 4

Ingredients

1 green, not quite ripe, mango
1 green crisp apple (Granny Smith), the core removed, peeled
85 g (3 oz) Parma ham (about 8-9 slices)
1 tsp red chilli, finely chopped
1 small crisp lettuce, broken into not too large pieces
1 tsp lime juice
1 tsp white wine vinegar
2 tbsp olive oil

½ tsp caster sugar
salt to taste

Cooking instructions

1. Peel the mango and using a potato peeler shave slivers off it until near its stone. Place them in a large salad bowl.
2. Peel and cut the apple into ½ inch (1 cm) dice. Add to the mango in the salad bowl.
3. Chop each slice of Parma ham into two pieces. Add to the salad bowl along with the finely chopped chilli and crisp pieces of lettuce.
4. Put into a small bottle the lime juice, white wine vinegar, sugar, salt and olive oil. Cork the bottle; shake it vigorously to emulsify the ingredients into a salad dressing. Pour into the salad bowl and, using your hands, gently mix all the ingredients. Serve immediately.

CARROT SALAD
Serves 4

Ingredients

4 large carrots, peeled and grated
2 thinly sliced spring onions
1 tbsp capers
1 tsp finely chopped red chilli
2 tbsp grape seed oil or sunflower oil
1 tsp fine caster sugar
1 tbsp freshly squeezed lime juice
1 tbsp coarsely chopped flat leaf parsley
salt to taste

Cooking instructions

1. Put the carrots, spring onions, capers and finely chopped chilli into a salad bowl.
2. Combine the grape seed or sunflower oil, lime juice, sugar and salt into a dressing. Add to the salad bowl and mix thoroughly. Garnish with the chopped parsley and serve.

RUSSIAN SALAD (A TRINI VERSION)
Serves 8-10 cold

Ingredients

900 g (2 lb) multipurpose or new potatoes, cooked (but not
    overcooked) and diced into ¾ inch (2 cm) cubes *
225 g (8 oz) carrots, cooked and diced into ½ inch (1¼ cm) cubes
115 g (4 oz) cooked beetroot, diced into ½ inch (1¼ cm) cubes
225 g (8 oz) green garden peas
8 hard-boiled free-range eggs, each cut into quarters
2 spring onions, finely chopped
300 ml (10 fl oz/½ pt) mayonnaise, preferably home-made (see
    Miscellany, p.229.)
2 tbsp whipped cream
1 tsp freshly ground black pepper
salt to taste
1 tbsp coarsely chopped parsley

* If new potatoes are being used, cook them in their skins and, once
  cooked, immediately put them into cold water for 2 minutes. Peel
  them while hot enough to handle, then dice them as required by this
  recipe.

Cooking instructions

1. Put all the vegetables into a serving dish and gently mix with your hands
    or a wooden spoon.
2. Whip the cream and mayonnaise together, then add to the serving dish
    along with the black pepper and hard-boiled eggs. With the wooden
    spoon, in gentle folding movements, integrate all the ingredients. Taste
    for seasoning and adjust if needed. Garnish with the chopped parsley.
    The salad is ready to be served.

TOMATO SALAD
Serves 4

Ingredients

12 medium-sized tomatoes, peeled, cut into quarters and the seeds
    removed
2 spring onions, sliced thinly and diagonally
1 tsp finely chopped chives
2 tbsp natural yoghurt
2 tbsp extra virgin olive oil
1 tsp balsamic vinegar
1 tsp caster sugar
1 tsp freshly ground black pepper
1 tbsp coarsely chopped basil
flaked sea salt to taste

Cooking instructions

1. Put the quartered tomatoes in a salad bowl along with the sliced spring
   onions. Mix together.
2. In a small mixing bowl, combine into a smooth salad dressing the yoghurt,
   finely chopped chives, olive oil, balsamic vinegar, caster sugar and black
   pepper. Add this dressing to the tomatoes.
3. Just before serving, sprinkle on 1 tsp of flaked sea salt and garnish with
   the coarsely chopped basil.

AT THE GREEN GROCER'S

He blushed
at the tomatoes'
plumpness;
preferred the ones
that gave a little
when squeezed;

felt an odd sense
of pride seeing
the firm cucumbers
in plastic skins.

He stopped short,
relaxing forefinger and thumb,
inches from the pert
raspberries.

Embarrassed,
he looked away;
observed a woman
peel a banana;
winced
as she bit into it.

Revised version
from *Behind the Carnival* (Smith/Doorstop Books)

KIDNEY BEANS AND RED PEPPER SALAD

Serves 4-6

Ingredients

450 g (1 lb) dried kidney beans, soaked overnight and cooked until soft;
   or 2 tins of cooked kidney beans, drained
2 red sweet peppers (capsicum), coarsely chopped
1 medium-sized red onion, sliced thinly into ½ rings
115 (4 oz) green runner beans, cooked and cut into thin strips
1 tbsp chopped parsley
4 tomatoes, peeled
2 tbsp extra virgin olive oil
1 garlic clove, coarsely chopped
½ tsp chilli powder
1 tsp balsamic vinegar
salt to taste

Cooking instructions

1. Combine in a salad bowl the kidney beans, sweet peppers, onion and strips of runner beans.

2. Score the tomatoes with a sharp knife and place them in a bowl. Pour enough boiling water to cover them. Leave them in the hot water for 5 minutes; drain the hot water away and replace it with cold water; peel the skins off the tomatoes after 1 minute, cut them into quarters.

3. Place in a food processor the tomatoes, olive oil, chopped garlic, chilli powder, balsamic vinegar and salt; process to a fine purée.

4. Add purée to the kidney beans. Thoroughly mix it in. Sprinkle over the mixture with the chopped parsley. Drizzle a little more olive oil over the salad if you wish, and serve.

CHICKEN AND RICE NOODLE SALAD
Serves 4

Ingredients

whole breast of a chicken, both halves thinly sliced and left for 30
   minutes in a marinade made with 1 lightly beaten egg white, 1 tbsp
   dry sherry, 1 generous tsp cornflour, salt, ¼ tsp black pepper and a
   dash of sesame oil, mixed together
4 tbsp groundnut oil for stir-frying the chicken
170 g (6 oz) fine rice noodles, cooked in boiling water for 1-2 minutes
   or until soft but firm to the bite and left to cool
3 free-range hard-boiled eggs, shelled and each cut into 6 wedges
85 g (3 oz) beansprouts, washed and drained
85 g (3 oz) thinly sliced French runner beans, cooked for 2 minutes in a
   small amount of boiling water, drained and set aside to cool
1 red sweet pepper (capsicum), thinly sliced
3 spring onions, their white ends thinly and diagonally sliced; and their
   green ends chopped for garnishing
1 garlic clove
2 slices of root ginger
½ green chilli, de-seeded and coarsely chopped
1 tsp brown sugar
juice of ½ lime
100 ml (4 fl oz) coconut milk
salt to taste

Cooking instructions

1. Divide marinated chicken into 4 roughly equal batches. Stir-fry each
   batch in 1 tbsp very hot groundnut oil for 1-2 minutes. Set aside each
   batch on kitchen paper towels to drain and become cool.

2. Mix together in a salad bowl the cooked French beans, red sweet pepper,
   beansprouts and spring onions. Add the cooked rice noodles and chicken;
   toss so that all the ingredients are well integrated.

3. Put in a food processor the garlic clove, root ginger, green chilli, sugar,
   lime juice, salt and coconut milk. Purée these ingredients to a smooth,
   creamy salad dressing. Pour over the chicken and noodles. Mix well
   together, garnish with the hard-boiled egg, chopped green spring onions
   and serve.

DESSERTS

One Cake Coming Up

KISS-KISS CHOCOLATE CAKE
Serves 8-12

Ingredients

125 g (4½ oz) butter, softened
3 free-range eggs
125 g (4½ oz) caster sugar
125 g (4½ oz) plain flour
1 tsp mixed spice
½ tsp bicarbonate of soda
75 ml (3 fl oz/4 tbsp) milk
100 g (3½ oz) dark chocolate
3 tbsp dark rum
2 tsp vanilla essence

Cooking instructions

1. Separate the egg yolks, reserving the whites for later use. Whisk the yolks and sugar until they become thick and foamy.

2. Break the chocolate into bits. Put them in a small saucepan and heat gently with the milk in a bain marie* until chocolate is melted.

3. Add butter to the melted chocolate and milk. Stir until smooth; then briskly stir in the beaten egg yolks. Add mixed spices and bicarbonate of soda to the flour and sift it into the chocolate mixture, stirring until smooth. Add in the rum and vanilla essence.

4. Whisk the egg whites until stiff; fold into the chocolate cake mix. Pour into a buttered and lined cake tin. Bake in a pre-heated oven at a temperature of 190°C/375°F/gas mark 5 for 45 minutes, or until a testing knife through the middle is withdrawn clean. Set aside to cool before serving.

*   A method of melting ingredients, or cooking individual sauces. Ingredients are put into a dish or small saucepan with a lid and placed into a larger saucepan of hot water on a gentle heat. Water in the larger saucepan must not be allowed to boil, in case the sauce being cooked curdles through being overheated, or water in the form of condensation gets into it and creates an undesirable result.

CARIBBEAN FRUIT SALAD

Serves 6-8

Ingredients

2 ripe mangoes, peeled, flesh sliced and slices cut again into smaller
   pieces
1 ripe, perfumed pineapple, peeled and diced
3 oranges, peeled and pulp removed
1 ripe paw-paw (papaya), peeled, de-seeded and diced
½ a small watermelon, seeds removed and flesh spooned out
170 g (6 oz) caster sugar
2 tbsp freshly squeezed lime juice
zest of 1 lime
50 ml (2 fl oz/3 tbsp) Caribbean rum

Cooking instructions

1. Put all the ingredients into a large salad bowl; cover and set aside for
    3-4 hours, preferably overnight in a refrigerator.
2. The fruit at this stage will have released their juices; stir gently before
    serving.

YOGHURT CAKE
Serves 8-12

Ingredients

140 g (5 oz) self-raising flour
85 g (3 oz) cornmeal or polenta
150 ml (5 fl oz/¼ pt) milk
150 ml (5 fl oz/¼ pt) natural yoghurt
150 g (5½ oz) caster sugar
1 free-range egg yolk
1 free-range egg
2 tbsp groundnut or sunflower oil
¼ tsp salt
¼ tsp bicarbonate of soda

Cooking instructions

1. Put all the ingredients in a large mixing bowl. Mix thoroughly with a wooden spoon. Set aside to rest for 15-20 minutes.
2. Pour into a well-greased cake tin of an accommodating size and bake in the oven at a temperature of 160°C/325°F/gas mark 3 for 45 minutes or until a testing knife is withdrawn quite clean. Remove from tin when cool enough to do so; but serve when cold.

PARLOUR SWEET BREAD
Makes 12 buns

Ingredients

225 g (8 oz) sugar
450 g (1 lb) plain flour
3 tsp baking powder
115 g (4 oz) margarine
110 g (4 oz) currants
1 grated coconut mixed with 250 ml (8 fl oz/ 1/3 pt) warm water
1 tsp vanilla essence
½ tsp salt

Cooking instructions

1. Mix flour and baking powder together in a large mixing bowl. Rub margarine
    into the flour.

2. Make a well in the flour and add sugar, grated coconut with its milk,
    vanilla, salt and currants. Mix well to form dough. Knead it until it becomes
    smooth and pliable (add a little flour if needed); this process ought to
    take 10 minutes. Cover with a clean, slightly damp cloth and set aside
    to relax for about 20 minutes.

3. Knead dough for another 5 minutes and divide into 12 equal pieces.
    Roll each piece into a ball and place on a greased and floured baking
    tray. Bake in the oven at a temperature of 160°C/325°F/gas mark 3
    for 30-45 minutes.

DROP-DONG COCONUT CAKES

Serves 8-16

Ingredients

85 g (3 oz) plain flour
½ tsp baking powder
I tsp ground cinnamon
I15 g (4 oz) fine caster sugar
I15 g (4 oz) desiccated coconut
150 ml (5 fl oz/¼ pt) milk
58 g (2 oz) butter
I free-range egg
I tsp vanilla essence

Cooking instructions

1. In a large mixing bowl, mix together the flour, cinnamon and baking powder.

2. In a small bowl, lightly whisk the egg, 50 ml (2 fl oz/3 tbsp) milk and I tsp vanilla essence. Add to the flour, cinnamon and baking powder and mix well. Set aside.

3. Gently heat the remaining 75 ml (3 fl oz/4 tbsp) milk, add butter. When the butter melts, add the sugar and desiccated coconut. Stir continuously until the sugar dissolves; add to the flour mixture and combine vigorously together with a wooden spoon. The consistency must be thick enough to keep its shape when full tablespoons of the mixture are dropped onto greased baking parchment.

4. Bake at an oven temperature of 180°C/350°F/gas mark 4 for 20-25 minutes until the cakes are golden brown.

CORN, CASSAVA, SWEET POTATO PONES
Each dish serves 8

These three sisters of the pone family are all sweet and tasty; but they are individuals in their own right. Methods of cooking are the same and they have ingredients in common. The differences in their ingredients, however, give them distinctive personalities.

Common ingredients

225 g (8 oz) grated coconut, or desiccated with 175 ml (6 fl oz) warm milk
225 g (8 oz) caster sugar
115 g (4 oz) melted butter
150 ml (5 fl oz/¼ pt) evaporated milk
1 tsp ground cinnamon
1 tsp vanilla essence

Different ingredients to add to each pone

Corn pone	Cassava pone	Sweet potato pone
350 g (12 oz) cornmeal	450 g (1 lb) grated cassava	350 g (12 oz) grated sweet potato
225 g (8 oz) grated pumpkin or butternut squash		170 g (6 oz) grated cassava
150 ml (5 fl oz/¼ pt) water		
¼ salt		

Cooking instructions

1. Combine all the ingredients in a large mixing bowl, stirring until the mixture looks well integrated.
2. Put the mixture in a well-greased ovenproof baking dish approximately 20 cm (8 inches) by 25 cm (10 inches) with a depth of 2 inches (5 cm). Bake in the oven at 180°C/350°F/gas mark 4 for 30 minutes, or until tested with a knife as being cooked through.
3. Set aside to cool. Divide into 8 equal portions while still in the baking dish before serving. May be eaten warm or cold.

SWEET PAIME

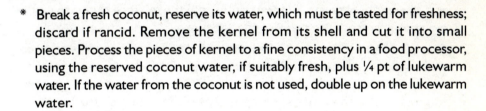

Ingredients

450 g (1 lb) polenta
225 g (8 oz) caster sugar
½ tsp ground white pepper
1 tsp ground cinnamon
1 finely processed fresh coconut *
250 g (8 oz) grated pumpkin or butternut squash
150 ml (5 fl oz/¼ pt) evaporated milk
2 tbsp melted sunflower margarine
1 tsp vanilla essence
2 tbsp sunflower oil
kitchen parchment (as replacement for banana leaves)
kitchen foil

* Break a fresh coconut, reserve its water, which must be tasted for freshness; discard if rancid. Remove the kernel from its shell and cut it into small pieces. Process the pieces of kernel to a fine consistency in a food processor, using the reserved coconut water, if suitably fresh, plus ¼ pt of lukewarm water. If the water from the coconut is not used, double up on the lukewarm water.

Cooking instructions

1. Blend in a deep mixing bowl: polenta, caster sugar, ground white pepper, cinnamon, finely processed coconut, grated pumpkin or squash, evaporated milk, melted margarine and vanilla essence. Mixture must be well-blended and not too soft; it should be able to slide slowly off a tablespoon held at a nearly vertical angle. Adjust texture accordingly with additional water or polenta if necessary.

2. Place an over-generous tbsp of the mixture on a rectangular piece of kitchen parchment 6 inches x 7 inches (16 cm x 18 cm) brushed with oil, and fold into a packet. Place the packet, folded side down, onto a piece of kitchen foil of a similar size as the parchment. Fold and seal. Repeat the process to produce the number of sweet paime required.

3. Put into boiling water. Cook for one hour. Drain and leave to cool a little, before unwrapping. Serve warm or cold.

SUGARCAKE
Makes about 20

Ingredients

100 ml (4 fl oz) water
225 g (8 oz) caster sugar
225 g (8 oz) grated coconut
¼ tsp cream of tartar
1 tsp almond or vanilla essence
food colouring (optional)

Cooking instructions

1. In a thick-bottomed saucepan, combine sugar and water, bring to the boil and cook until it is bubbling furiously as syrup. Add the grated coconut and the cream of tartar. Stir constantly until the mixture begins to come away readily from the sides of the saucepan.

2. Remove the saucepan from the heat, add the almond or vanilla essence and colouring (if using) and beat vigorously for 2-3 minutes. Measure out on lightly greased baking parchment tablespoonfuls of the sugarcake mixture; leave them to set completely before eating or storing them away.

COCONUT VENDOR

DRINKS

Go On, Have a Drink

THE BOIS BANDE REMEDY

Man, dohn mess wid *bois bande*,
de bush-doctor's remedy.

It may look like *mauby bark*,
buh dat's to fool yuh. It got de knack

of being over-enthusiastic,
always ready to perform its magic trick.

I once knew ah sagaboy;
fuh him ah woman was like ah toy.

But soon his manhood stop firing,
his effort to revive it was tiring

and yes, he needed the remedy;
buh he took too much *bois bande*.

He had to be hospitalised
to bring him back to human size.

AVOCADO PEP

Ingredients

1 ripe but firm avocado (green smooth-skin ones are best)
250 ml (8 fl oz/$^1/_3$ pt) cold water (one-third)
400 ml (14 fl oz/$^2/_3$ pt) coconut milk (two-thirds)
juice of 1 freshly squeezed lime
1 tsp Worcester sauce
50 ml (2 fl oz/3 tbsp) vodka or gin (optional)
Tabasco to taste
salt to taste

Making instructions

Put all the ingredients into a blender. Blend until smooth, refrigerate and serve chilled.

Make a friend of this drink and feel good!

BAD-JOHN

The old-time name for a hooligan or a ruffian. The nickname of an actual street tough, one John Archer, who plagued the courts in the first decade of the 20th century.

Ingredients

1 bottle Guinness (export quality)
1 free-range egg
150 ml (5 fl oz/$^1/_4$ pt) condensed milk
75 ml (3 fl oz/4 tbsp) Scotch whisky

Making instructions

Put all the ingredients in a blender. Blend until smooth and serve with crushed ice.

BROWN SKIN GYAL

Ingredients

50 ml (3 tbsp) rum
40 ml (2 tbsp) single cream
I tbsp instant coffee
3 tbsp caster sugar
I tsp water
hot water

Making instructions

1. Put instant coffee, sugar and water in a bowl. Mix thoroughly with a spoon. Continue mixing more vigorously until the sugar is melted into the coffee, then begin to beat it into a mixture that looks like a beige-coloured mousse.

2. Put about I measure (50 ml/3 tbsp) rum in a footed glass mug. Add I generous tbsp mousse to it.

3. Pour hot water (not boiling water) gently through the mousse, without stirring, so that it rises ¾ of the way up the glass mug. Mix 2 drops of vanilla essence into 40 ml (2 tbsp) single cream; pour it gently onto the back of a clean tablespoon allowing it to flow into the risen coffee mousse. The cream will rise to the surface. There should be three coloured layers from the bottom of the glass mug upwards: the brown of the coffee, the beige of the mousse and the pinkish white of the cream. As you drink you will find the temperature differences interesting. This coffee mousse mixture could make 2 servings.

Smooth and seductive!

GINGER STING

Go easy with this quiet one!

Ingredients

300 ml (10 fl oz/½ pt) ginger cordial
150 ml (5 fl oz/¼ pt) light rum
2 tbsp freshly squeezed lime juice
peel of ½ a lime
soda water

Making instructions

1. Mix in a glass jug: ginger cordial, rum and lime juice.
2. Pour a desirable measure of the ginger cordial mixture into a glass of crushed ice. Add soda water, stir and serve with a straw, garnished with lime peel.

JOHNNY'S ICED TEA

Ah go cool yuh dong wen yuh need it.

Ingredients

1 litre (35 fl oz/1¾ pt) cold tea
   brewed at medium strength
300 ml (10 fl oz/½ pt) simple syrup
   (see p. 229)
150 ml (5 fl oz/¼ pt) rum
¼ tsp vanilla essence (optional)
juice freshly squeezed from ½ a lemon

Making instructions

1. Pour the litre of cold tea into a glass serving jug. Add the simple syrup and stir until the syrup becomes an integral part of the cold tea.
2. Add the rum, lemon and vanilla essence (if being used), stir and pour into glasses with cubes of ice. Serve garnished with a twist of lemon.

MAMMIE'S GINGER BEER

Ingredients

450 g (1 lb) root ginger, scraped clean, washed and coarsely grated
900 g (2 lb) brown granulated sugar
115 g (4 oz) long grain rice
5 cloves
1 inch (2½ cm) length of cinnamon bark
1 tbsp cream of tartar
4 litres (7 pts) boiling water
the peel of 2 limes

Making instructions

1. In a very large earthenware or glass jar put 450 g (1 lb) of the granulated sugar and all the rest of the dry ingredients. Pour the boiling water onto it, cover and allow it to steep for 3 days, preferably leaving the jar in the sun.
2. Strain the liquid into another glass or earthenware jar through a double layer of muslin placed in a sieve, pressing the solids with a spoon to make sure all the flavour is extracted. Stir in the remaining 450 g (1 lb) of sugar until dissolved, cover and set aside for another day.
3. Strain again through muslin, bottle and refrigerate.

MANGO MASQUERADE

Dohn leh dis drink fool yuh!

Ingredients

1 very ripe mango
150 ml (5 fl oz/¼ pt) simple syrup
175 ml (6 fl oz) rum
150 ml (5 fl oz/¼ pt) single cream
1 dash Angostura Bitters

Making instructions

Put all the ingredients in a blender. Blend at high speed and serve in glasses with crushed ice.

MAUBY

Good on a hot day with lots of ice. As a boy I loved it with sweet bread.

Ingredients

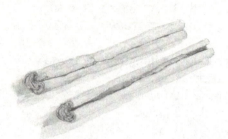

1 tbsp crushed mauby bark
1 tsp dried orange peel
3 whole cloves
½ a cinnamon stick
1 star anise
450 g (1 lb) light brown sugar
Angostura bitters

Cooking instructions

1. Simmer in 250 ml (8 fl oz) water for 5 minutes the above ingredients with the exception of the sugar and Angostura bitters. Set aside to cool.

2. When cool, add 2 litres of water, sugar and 2 dashes of Angostura bitters. Mix well until the sugar is dissolved, then strain into sterilised bottles and refrigerate. Mauby stored in this way will last for 2 weeks.

3. Dilute to desired tastes, serve with ice. Great on a hot day.

NENNIE'S PONCHACREM

A real Christmas treat.

Ingredients

4 free-range eggs
1 tin condensed milk
1 tin evaporated milk
175 ml (6 fl oz) good light rum
1 tsp Angostura Bitters
½ tsp vanilla essence
½ tsp grated nutmeg
zest of 1 lime

Making instructions

1. Blend the eggs and lime zest in a blender at high speed for a few seconds.

2. Add the rest of the ingredients and continue to blend to a creamy texture. Pour into a jug and leave in the refrigerator. Serve cold.

PISTASH PUNCH

Slips smoothly down your throat.

Ingredients

450 ml (15 fl oz/¾ pt) milk
85 g (3 oz) smooth peanut butter
3 tbsp icing sugar
100 ml (4 fl oz/¹/₅ pt) single cream
3 tbsp rum
1 dash Angostura Bitters

Making instructions

Put all the ingredients in a blender and blend until smooth and creamy.
Place in the refrigerator. Serve cold.

SUNNY BOY

Puts a smile on your face and warmth in your heart. Serves 2-4

Ingredients

1 tin (400 ml/14 fl oz) coconut milk
1 tin condensed milk (about 375 g)
450 ml (15 fl oz/¾ pt) pure orange juice
150 ml (5 fl oz/¼ pt) rum
50 ml (2 fl oz/3 tbsp) Cointreau

Making instructions

1. Put all the ingredients in a blender. Blend at high speed.
2. Pour onto crushed ice in a glass, garnish with a slice of orange and serve
   with a drinking straw.

TRINI EGG NOG
A tonic to put a sparkle in your eyes. Serves 2

Ingredients

2 free-range eggs
575 ml (20 fl oz/1 pt) full cream milk
150 ml (5 fl oz/¼ pt) light rum
1 tsp vanilla essence
1 dash Angostura Bitters
55 g (2 oz) caster sugar
¼ tsp grated nutmeg
peel of 1 lime

Making instructions

1. Beat eggs in a bowl along with the peel of 1 lime. Remove the lime peel.
2. Put the beaten eggs and the rest of the ingredients in a blender. Blend until creamy-smooth and serve.

TRINI RUM PUNCH

Trini rum punch may be made to any strength desired; and lends itself to experimentation. The general proportions of the ingredients are:

For a strong punch

4 measures of strong
3 of sweet
2 of sour
1 of weak
Angostura Bitters

The actual ingredients are: rum for strong, simple syrup for sweet, lime juice for sour and crushed ice for weak. The first three ingredients with the Angostura are shaken together and poured into a glass of crushed ice and garnished with a slice of lime. Treat this one with respect.

For a weaker punch

1 measure of sour
2 of sweet
3 of strong
4 of weak
Angostura Bitters

The actual ingredients are the same as above with the exception of the '4 of weak', which could be a combination of fruit juices, often with slices of desired fruit added to it. This weaker punch is gentler but still demands a certain respect.

BALSAMIC SYRUP

50 ml (2 fl oz/3 tbsp) water
75 ml (3 fl oz/4 tbsp) balsamic vinegar
170 g (6 oz) granulated sugar

In a small saucepan on medium heat stir sugar and water until dissolved; then add the balsamic vinegar. Stir until well integrated. Boil to 107°C/225°F. This syrup can be used for making salad dressings and as an addition to sauces.

BEURRE MANIÉ

Mix equal proportions of softened butter and plain flour together to make a smooth paste. Small knobs of this mixture could be added to simmering liquid, soups, sauces and stews. Simmer for 3 minutes to allow the flour to cook.

BOUQUET GARNI

This is a selection of aromatic herbs used to flavour stocks and sauces. Tie together in a small bundle the following herbs: 1 sprig of rosemary, thyme, parsley, bay leaf, or any other herb that you desire for your stock, soup or sauce. A selection of dried herbs may also be tied into a small bit of muslin and used as a bouquet garni.

COCONUT MILK

Take one whole husked dried coconut with its three eyes intact, weighing a little heavy in the palm of your hand, and sounding full of water when shaken. Some cooks recommend the warming of the coconut in a hot oven to allow the hard shell to come away easily from the kernel when the nut is broken. I have never tried this; but what I do is simply to crack the coconut shell open with a hammer and drain its water into a glass or cup to be used later if it is sweetish to the taste; otherwise, discard it if it is not to your liking. Still using the hammer, I then break up the coconut into manageable pieces and carefully remove the white kernel with an oyster knife.

The next stage is to rinse the pieces of coconut and coarsely chop them into smaller pieces. Put the pieces in a liquidiser/food processor along with the reserved water and about 450 ml (¾ pt) of warm water and process. Drain through a strainer lined with muslin. Squeeze as much milk through as you can, pressing with your fist; then, removing the residue-filled muslin, continue expressing the milk with a wringing, twisting motion. If you so desire, a little more warm water could be added to the residue and squeezed to extract a little more milk, albeit much thinner in consistency.

The above method is fun; but if you haven't got the time, a commercially produced coconut milk is conveniently sold in many supermarkets.

HUSKING COCONUT

CURRY POWDERS

A basic curry powder

2 tsp turmeric powder
1 tsp cumin seeds
2 tsp coriander seeds
1-2 tsp chilli flakes
1 tsp peppercorns
3 cloves
1 inch (2½ cm) cinnamon stick

Dry roast (without burning) in a frying pan on medium heat the above spices, with the exception of the turmeric powder. Note: When the aroma begins to rise from the roasting spices, it is time to remove them from the heat. Put all the roasted spices along with the 2 tsp turmeric powder in a coffee grinder reserved only for the purpose of grinding spices. Grind to a curry powder.

JOHN'S ROBUST CURRY POWDER

(Will make enough for 2-3 curry cooking sessions)

1 tsp mustard seeds
1 tsp chilli flakes
3 tsp coriander seeds
2 tsp cumin seeds
1 tsp black peppercorns
3 cloves
½ tsp fenugreek
1 tbsp dried curry leaves
1 inch (2½ cm) cinnamon stick
1 inch (2½ cm) piece of galangal
1 tbsp turmeric powder
1 tsp paprika

Dry roast (without burning) in a frying pan on medium heat all the spices, except the turmeric powder, paprika and dried curry leaves. Remove from the heat as soon as the spices begin to give off their aroma. Put all the roasted spices along with the turmeric powder, paprika and dried curry leaves in your spice-designated coffee grinder and grind to a powder.

These curry powders could be made into curry pastes with the addition of a little oil and water and a teaspoon of tomato purée (optional).

JOHN'S MASALA

2 inches (5 cm) cinnamon stick
7 cloves
2 tsp black peppercorns
1 tbsp cumin seeds
½ tsp fennel seeds

Dry-roast the spices in a frying pan on medium heat. Take care not to burn them; as soon as the aroma begins to rise, remove from the heat and subject them to vigorous pounding using a mortar and pestle until transformed to a powder. There is your masala. An alternative method for making the roasted spices into the masala powder is the use of a spice-designated coffee grinder.

LEMON/LIME WATER

Lemon water or lime water is habitually used as a means of cleansing meat or fish before marinating. To make lemon or lime water, simply add the juice of 1 or 2 lemons to 150 ml (5 fl oz/¼ pt) clean fresh water. This mixture can be made weaker or stronger if required.

MARINADES

Growing up in Trinidad as a boy I observed how my parents seasoned (marinated) meat with herbs and spices, which included the infamous Scotch bonnet pepper, before cooking it. Later on I understood it to be a traditional method of cooking, which probably harked back to the days when refrigeration was not a readily available facility for poor people in the islands. It was certainly a way of preserving meat for a short while in tropical temperatures. This method of seasoning was also used as a means of tenderising meat and complementing its taste. This treatment given to meat characteristically defines a major element of Caribbean gastronomy.

In my view marinades/seasonings may be categorised as: dry marinades, wet marinades and runny marinades (for steeping large cuts of meat).

Dry marinades are made with spices gently dry-roasted and ground to a powder, using your mortar and pestle or spice-designated coffee grinder, which is then rubbed into the meat and put aside, wrapped in cling film, in the refrigerator for half an hour to two hours for the seasoning to take effect.

Wet marinades are made using the powdered roasted spices into which are pounded fresh herbs, garlic, onion, salt, oil and an alcohol, if desired, to make a paste which is then rubbed into the meat leaving it to marinate for two hours or overnight.

A runny marinade is made using liquid ingredients singly or in a mixture, depending on the strength of flavour of the liquid ingredients such as wine, soy sauce, lemon juice, lime juice, pepper sauce or vinegar. In addition, crushed or finely chopped onion and garlic may be added to the liquid. In this method the meat is steeped: completely covered with the marinade.

The making of seasonings or marinades leaves room for creative flexibility. It is like being a painter in the process of mixing paint. Consider the herb and spice ingredients as the variety of colours you have at your disposal. With the knowledge of individual spice ingredients and what they can do, and having an idea of the taste effects you want, creative experimentation in a made-to-purpose marinade can be satisfying, to say the least. The following is a list of seasoning ingredients, a few of which may be considered unusual. The fun is using them in various combinations, or singly as spices in their own right:

Onion, garlic, thyme, parsley, celery, coriander leaves (a substitute for the Trinidad herb, *shado beni*), coriander seeds, chives, dill, tarragon, bay leaf, root ginger, powdered ginger, black pepper, cinnamon, cloves, allspice, cumin, chillies, Scotch bonnet pepper, turmeric powder, paprika, salt, vinegar, lemon juice, lime juice, rum, port, vermouth, Angostura Bitters, molasses, honey, sugar, oils, green paw-paw skin, fennel herb.

BACCRA JOHNNIE CHICKEN MARINADE

Ingredients

1 clove garlic
1 spring onion (Caribbean chives)
1 tbsp fresh thyme
2 tsp black peppercorns
½ de-seeded, finely minced, small hot red chilli (optional)
1 tbsp chopped parsley
2 tsp coarse sea salt
5 fl oz (¼ pt) white rum

Making instructions

1. Roast for 1 minute in a frying pan over medium heat the black peppercorns
   and coarse sea salt, then grind to a powder using a mortar and pestle.*
2. Add the garlic, spring onion, thyme, parsley and chilli. Continue to pound
   these ingredients into a paste. Stir in the rum. The marinade is now
   ready to be rubbed into the chicken. Marinate chicken for at least 30
   minutes before cooking.

* Alternatively, the grinding of peppercorns and coarse salt to a powder
may be done with a coffee grinder designated to the grinding of spices.

'M'S CHICKEN MARINADE

Ingredients

1 tbsp black peppercorns
2 tsp coarse sea salt
2 tsp coriander seeds
3 cloves
½ inch (1 cm) cinnamon stick
2 garlic cloves
½ red hot chilli
1 tbsp chopped tarragon
2 tbsp rum
½ tsp Angostura bitters
2 tbsp olive oil
1 tbsp balsamic syrup (optional, see p.221)

The making

1. Dry roast in a frying pan the black peppercorns, coarse sea salt, coriander seeds, cloves and cinnamon stick. When they begin to release their aroma, put them into a mortar and pound to a powder.

2. Add the garlic, red hot chilli and tarragon. Continue to crush to a paste.

3. Pour into this paste the rum, Angostura bitters, olive oil and balsamic syrup. Stir to integrate. It is now ready to be rubbed into the chicken.

FISH MARINADE

Mainly for large meaty fish like shark, swordfish, bonito, grouper, cut into chunky steaks 1½ inches (4 cm) thick.

½ tsp fennel seeds
½ tsp black peppercorns
1 tsp grated ginger
2 plump, finely chopped garlic cloves
1 tbsp finely chopped dill
1 tbsp powdered turmeric
2 tbsp freshly squeezed lime juice
2 tsp fine sea salt
1 tbsp sunflower or corn oil
3 tbsp gin
1 tsp finely minced Scotch bonnet pepper (optional)

Dry-roast the fennel seeds and black peppercorns (without burning them) on a medium heat until the aroma begins to be released. Using a mortar and pestle crush the roasted spices to a powder. Add the remaining ingredients, with the exception of the lime juice and oil, and continue crushing to produce a paste. Stir in the lime juice and oil. This marinade is what I call the wet variety; and the addition of white wine or vermouth to it in sufficient quantities, as a means of saturating the fish, is what I refer to as liquid marinade.

For a lighter fish marinade follow the same method using the following ingredients:

1 finely chopped garlic clove
1 tsp grated ginger
1 tbsp lime juice
1 tbsp sunflower oil
salt to taste

MAYONNAISE

A cold emulsified sauce made with egg yolks and oil blended together with an egg whisk or electric mixer. It is usually flavoured with mustard, salt, black pepper and vinegar.

Put the following ingredients into a medium-sized mixing bowl: 2 free-range egg yolks, 2 tsp white wine or cider vinegar, freshly squeezed lemon juice, salt, 1 tsp Dijon mustard, white pepper. Mix vigorously these ingredients. Blend in about 300 ml (10 fl oz/½ pt) extra virgin oil, drop by drop initially, adding also a few drops of vinegar; and as the mixture increases in volume, add the oil in thin trickles. Continue blending and it will begin to emulsify, become lighter in colour and increase in volume. At this stage, taste and adjust seasoning and flavour ready to be used.

SEASONED FLOUR

Used when frying fish or meat. Usually fish or meat is floured lightly, dipped into beaten egg, rolled in breadcrumbs and placed into the frying pan.

2 tbsp plain flour
1 tsp freshly ground black pepper
1 tsp salt
2 tsp dried thyme, or any dried herb you wish (dill is suitable for fish)
½ tsp powdered fennel (suitable for fish)
2 tsp turmeric powder (suitable for fish) (optional)

Put all the ingredients in a plastic bag and shake thoroughly to mix together. Double or treble the ingredients to suit the quantity of meat or fish. To flour lightly, shake the meat or fish, a piece at a time, in the plastic bag of seasoned flour.

SIMPLE SYRUP

100 ml (4 fl oz) water
115 g (4 oz) sugar

Boil the water in a small stainless steel saucepan. Add the sugar to the boiling water stirring until the sugar is completely dissolved. Boil to 107°C/225°F.

JL'S MENU COOKING GRID

From time to time I am invited to tutor on poetry courses at the Ted Hughes Arvon Centre, Lumb Bank. On these residential courses all the food is provided as raw ingredients and groups of students take a turn in cooking it. The last night of the course is usually the Friday which is marked by a celebratory feast, and an atmospheric turbulence of creative excitement, in the most positive way imaginable.

Whenever I tutor on Arvon courses, it has become a self-imposed custom of mine to take on the responsibility of organising the cooking of this feast; and, happily, I am never short of helpers. Usually the menu for this feast is a modest four courses. The numbers sitting at table are between twenty and twenty-five, including tutors and Centre staff. Invariably there are vegetarians, which might include one or two vegans, among the students. In these circumstances, organising the cooking is evidently of vital importance.

Necessity, it is said, is the mother of invention; and so it most certainly was on my first Arvon cooking venture. It occurred to me that a formulaic approach in what I call a *menu cooking grid*, could be a great help in keeping attention, not only on the sequential order of the cooking process, but also on the coordinated timing of the various dishes which comprise the menu.

I designed a grid with enough space in each rectangle for noting culinary processes: in the top row of the grid, I write in each rectangle the name of a dish in the menu. The stages in the cooking process for each dish are written in the column below. (Please refer to diagram opposite.)

This format also facilitates the kitchen management: I allocate jobs to helper-cooks by marking their initials against cooking stages in the grid. The grid is then stuck onto the wall in the kitchen. Each student helper-cook, by consulting the displayed grid, knows what to do at a glance during the period of preparation. This approach lends itself to organising beforehand the cooking ingredients and all the tools necessary for the successful cooking of each dish. The actual cooking times and coordinated sequences are given as direct instructions so that all dishes are correctly cooked and served on time.

Another advantage of this sort of planning, bearing in mind the number of guests, and with an eye on economy, is the making of a shopping list. I hasten to add, this is just my way of working in a kitchen with many helper-cooks; but I do also use this grid when I am cooking at home for a large number of invited dinner guests. Cooking, being a creative activity, remains open to many different approaches suitable to the diverse temperaments and creative inclinations of cooks. I have found that the 'menu cooking grid' works very well for me. It may work for you too, why not try it, especially when you have family helpers.

JL'S MENU COOKING GRID

Stage	Smoked Fish Accra	King Fish in Tomato Sauce	Plain Boiled Rice	Caribbean Fruit Salad
1	Poach the smoked fish. Cool in cold water.	Clean and wash fish slices.	Wash rice.	Wash fruit.
2	Flake fish.	Make marinade, add fish to it. Set aside.	Add to salted boiling water.	Cut into different sizes.
3	Slice onions, thinly. Finely mince garlic and herbs.	Flour fish; fry in hot oil. Put on kitchen paper towel.	Cook for 7-10 minutes.	Add sugar & rum to fruit in bowl.
4	Make a batter. Add fish & vegetables to it.	FOR SAUCE Peel and chop tomatoes, onion, garlic and ginger.	Add butter or oil. Ready to serve.	Set aside in the fridge. Stir to integrate.
5	Leave in fridge for 30 minutes.	Fry onion. Add garlic, stir. Add ginger, tomatoes, stock.		
6	Fry in hot oil; drain.	Add fish to sauce; lower heat. Stir, taste, season.		

For full cooking procedure, please see individual recipes.

DEFINITIONS

Angostura bitters: A reddish brown bitters made in Trinidad and mainly used for flavouring cocktails and pink gins. It may also be used in very small quantities in cooking.

Breadfruit: A large spherical fruit reputed to have been brought to the Caribbean Islands by Captain Bligh of the *Bounty*. It has a pimply skin, green when mature but yellow-brown when ripe. It is cooked as a vegetable and is rich in carbohydrate and vitamins A, B and C.

Browning: A dark brown liquid used as a colouring agent for the famous Christmas black cake. It is made by adding a proportionate quantity of water to caramelising sugar.

Cassava (*manioc*): A long, hard-fleshed root vegetable with a stiff leathery skin and white flesh. Its starch content is very high. There are two types of cassava, bitter and sweet. Sweet cassava is cooked as a vegetable by boiling; the bitter cassava is grated and the starch extracted from it. Cassava farine is made from the residue.

Coal pot: A small, round, cast-iron, charcoal-burning, open stove, consisting of a container bowl with a removable grate in its bottom, supported on a squat neck with an opening for air and scraping ash away.

Corned fish: Fish filleted, salted and dried in the sun.

Cornmeal: Dried grains of maize which are ground into a flour; commercially, it is called polenta.

Dasheen: A vegetable tuber with a brown hairy skin. It is rich in starch and is cooked by boiling. The stem and heart-shaped leaves of the plant are used for making callaloo.

Eddoe: A root vegetable similar to the dasheen, but much smaller, about the size of a potato. It is slimy when peeled, but cooked it is smooth-textured and much favoured in making soups.

Farine: A coarse-grained meal made by stirring the residue of grated bitter cassava (after the poisonous juice has been expressed out of it) in a large cast-iron pot over a fire until it is dried out while retaining its whitish colour.

Green fig: Mature, unripe banana.

Ground provisions: A collective name for the variety of starchy tubers grown in the ground which, in the days of slavery, was set aside on sugar plantations to enable slaves to grow their own food. These days the term is extended to include all garden produce.

Lanty peas: Brown lentils.

Lemon water: A mixture of lemon juice and water which is used as a cleansing liquid for meat and fish. See Miscellany p. 224

Lime water: A mixture of lime juice and water which is used as a cleansing liquid for meat and fish.

Okra (okro *T'dad*; ladyfingers *Eng*): A young, green pod about 4 inches (10 cm) long whose flesh and seeds are slimy. It is ridged and pointed at one end. It is used as a vegetable ingredient in the making of callaloo.

Paw Paw (papaya): A fruit whose flesh is sweet and pale orange when ripe with small dark seeds scattered centrally in it. Both the leaves and fruit when green contain papain, an enzyme that digests protein. For this reason, it is used as a meat tenderiser.

Pigeon Pea: A seed-bearing pod whose seeds vary from pale green to yellow; they resemble garden peas in shape and size. Pigeon peas are used in soups and the well-loved 'rice and peas', especially in Trinidad.

Plantain: A large green form of the banana which never ripens in the same way as does a sweet banana. When a plantain is ripe the skin turns dark brown, almost black. Plantains must always be cooked; boiled when green or just ripe, fried when quite ripe. Green plantains can be made into crisps.

Salt fish (*bacalao*): Salted, dried cod.

Sweet potato: A sweetish, edible tuber with a pink- or brown-coloured skin and cream or grey flesh. It is part of what is collectively called 'ground provisions'.

Sweet corn: Maize.

Tannia: A tuber about 4 to 5 inches (10-12 cm) long with a coarse pinkish texture when boiled as a vegetable; part of 'ground provisions'.

Zaboca: Avocado.

STORE

To prevent the index from growing beyond a useful size, listed below are some of the items which are either assumed to be in most kitchens; are recommended store ingredients for Trini cooking; or ingredients that are used so frequently that indexing some of them is pointless.

Staples
Chillies (usually Scotch bonnet), chives, fresh coriander, garlic, lemons, limes, milk, onions, pepper sauce (Encona), sea salt, shallots, sugar (brown cane), tomato puree, stock cubes (vegetable, chicken) tinned coconut milk, tinned tomatoes.

Oils & fats
Butter, corn oil, lard, margarine, olive oil, sesame oil, sunflower oil.

Baking
baking powder, bicarbonate of soda, cornflour, cream of tartar, dried or fresh yeast, plain flour, self-raising flour.

Flavourings
Angostura bitters, balsamic vinegar, brown ale, cider vinegar, Dijon mustard, gin, Guinness, lager, rum (dark and white), sherry, sherry vinegar, soy sauce, vermouth, whisky, wine (red and white), wine vinegar

Herbs
Basil, bay leaf, coriander seed, cumin seed, dill, fennel seed, oregano, parsley, rosemary, tarragon, thyme. In particular fresh chives, coriander, parsley, spring onions and thyme occur in so many of the recipes they are worth keeping in pots on your window sill or in plentiful supply in your garden.

Spices
Allspice, black pepper, cardamons, chilli flakes, cinnamon, cloves, curry powder, five-spice powder, garam masala, ground ginger, mustard powder, mustard seed, nutmeg, paprika, star anise, turmeric.

INDEX OF RECIPES BY TITLE

INDEX OF POEMS

INDEX OF INGREDIENTS AND METHODS

Cucumber
  seafood salad, 186
  souse, 35
Currants
  parlour sweet bread, 204
  Trinidad Christmas cake, 198
Curry
  a Trini's curried lamb's kidneys, 107
  curried beef, 195
  curried chicken thighs, 67
  curried crab meat with herb dumplings, 44
  curried fish in coconut milk, 52
  curried fish in puff pastry, 46
  curried goat, 109
  curried mussels, 48
  curried pork, 117
  curry powders, 223
  vegetable curry, 171

Dasheen, 232
  callaloo, 127
Desserts
  Caribbean fruit salad, 202
  cassava pone, 206
  corn pone, 206
  drop-dong coconut cake, 205
  kiss-kiss chocolate cake, 201
  parlour sweet bread, 204
  sweet paime, 207
  sweet potato pone, 206
  sugarcake, 208
  Trinidad Christmas cake, 198
  yoghurt cake, 203
Dill
  Trini fish broth, 142
Drinks
  avocado pep, 212
  bad-john, 212
  brown-skin gyal, 213
  ginger sting, 214
  Johnny's iced tea, 214
  Mammie's ginger beer, 215
  mango masquerade, 215
  mauby, 216
  Nennie's ponchacrem, 215
  pistash punch, 217
  sunny boy, 217
  Trini egg nog, 218
  Trini rum punch, 218
Dumplings
  boyoboy, 161
  coconut smoked fish with cornmeal
    dumplings, 41
  cream of pigeon peas soup, 135
  curried crab meat with herb dumplings, 44

Eddoe, 232
  sancoche, 139
Eggs
  a Trini fried rice, 177
  black pudding breakfast pattie, 20
  buljol, 14
  cheeky yam souffle, 163
  chicken and rice noodle salad, 194
  creole fried rice, 174
  Dubroyd chicken, 78
  nennie's ponchacrem, 216
  puff-up breadfruit, 150
  rice croquettes, 18
  ripe plantain gambage, 158
  Russian salad (a Trini version), 190
  Trini egg nog, 218

Evaporated milk
  pones, 206
  sweet paime, 207

Fennel (bulb)
  fish bacchanal, 50
Fennel (herb)
  saltfish with okra and tomatoes, 61
  sulking mackerel, 62
Fish(see haddock, kingfish, mackerel,
monkfish, snapper, tuna and whitefish)
  bacchanal, 50
  char-grilled tuna, 56
  coconut smoked fish with cornmeal
    dumplings, 41
  curried fish in coconut milk, 46
  curried fish in puff pastry, 46
  escoveitch, 54
  green fig curry, 149
  JL's fish chowder, 144
  one-pot steamed fish and rice, 58
  roe rolls, 17
  saltfish accras, 15
  saltfish buljol, 14
  saltfish with okra and tomatoes, 61
  smoked fish pasta, 183
  smoked haddock accras, 15
  smoked haddock buljol, 14
  stock, 48
  sulking mackerel, 62
  Tobago fish tea & Trini fish broth, 142
Flour, seasoned, 229
Flour
  coconut smoked fish, 42
  doubles, 32
  float, 16
  fry bakes, 19
  mash yam fritters, 165
  roti, 29
  sweet potato pancakes, 155
Fruit
  Caribbean fruit salad, 202
  mango and apple salad with parma ham, 188
  mango and veg salad, 188

Gammon (see Bacon)
Gin
  avocado pep, 212
  fish marinade, 228
  sulking mackerel, 62
Ginger
  curried chicken thighs, 67
  beef sagaboy, 94
  ginger sting, 214
  Mammie's ginger beer, 215
  sulking mackerel, 62
Goat
  curried goat, 109
Green bananas, 232
  green fig curry, 149
  Tobago fish tea & Trini fish broth, 142
Green figs (see Green bananas)
Ground provision, 232
Guinness
  bad-john, 212

Haddock
  curried fish in coconut milk, 52
Haddock (smoked)
  accras, 15
  buljol, 14